MS, Me a⌐

Ginny Faith

GILEAD
B O O K S
PUBLISHING

Gilead Books Publishing
Corner Farm
West Knapton
Malton
North Yorkshire YO17 8JB UK
www.GileadBooksPublishing.com

First published in Great Britain, March 2017
2 4 6 8 10 9 7 5 3 1

Copyright © Ginny Faith 2017

British Library Cataloguing-in-Publication Data:
A catalogue record for this book is available from the British
Library.

ISBN: 978-0-9932090-8-6

Scripture quotations are taken from the Holy Bible, New Living
Translation, copyright ©1996, 2004, 2007 by Tyndale House
Foundation. Used by permission of Tyndale House Publishers, Inc.,
Carol Stream, Illinois 60188. All rights reserved.

The publisher makes every effort to ensure that the papers used
in our books are made from trees that have been legally sourced
from well-managed and credibly certified forests by using a
printer awarded FSC & PEFC chain of custody certification.

Cover design: Nathan Ward

Contents

Acknowledgments

I would like to thank the Lord first, for showering me with His love. He never gave up on me and continues to bless me to this day.

I would like to thank Joe and Suzi King for all their hard work, teaching me, praying over me seeking healing and deliverance. They have given me so much, helping me to start my healing journey. I am thankful for the prayers I have used in this book from the Healing School materials of 2004.

I would also like to thank all my family, my husband and boys and especially my Mum and Dad, for giving me their love and support over the years. I am really blessed to belong to such a loving and helpful family. I would like to thank my Church family and friends too. So many people have blessed me with encouragement. Some with practical help too. Some with their welcoming smile and hugs, all blessing me.

I would also like to thank the kind people in Normanton who have blessed me by smiling at me, and complete strangers who have gone out of their way to help me when needed. All this makes me feel I am well and truly blessed – which of course I am! I am still living in pain, but it is not of the same magnitude and no longer is the dominant force in my life. God is, and I am so much happier as a result! I look forward in great anticipation to see what He will do next!

Introduction

I wanted to write this book, because I knew it could help others. I have found over the MS years, that suffering people often have no hope. My hope comes from Jesus, and seeing Him heal me time and again, how He can make new what the medical profession have given up on. All the poor decisions I have made in my life, are not too hard for Him to resolve. He always makes a way through, and often makes something beautiful. Although I found it difficult sharing painful times from my past, the Lord spoke into my spirit; "It's not about you, it's all about Jesus." I still have many problems with the MS, and yet I know that the manifestation of my complete healing from the Lord will come soon. I look forward with great expectancy and joy, to see what He will do next.

Ginny

1 – A Nightmare Reality

I am not sure precisely when the pins and needles began in my hands. Unfortunately I did not keep a note of exactly when it was, until the end of May 2003. In the last week of May, my husband, boys and I, went on a family holiday to Italy with my in-laws. I remember looking at my hands and wondering what the symptoms of pins and needles meant. They had been intermittent at first. Now on holiday, the symptoms were permanent. In spite of this, we all enjoyed a lovely holiday.

We returned home and my husband and I went back to work. I had worked part-time since having children. Gradually over a three-month period, the symptoms spread. The pins and needles remained in my hands and then began in my feet. After the feet, they reached into my ankles and then started to creep up my legs. More disturbing was the numbness that began in my feet. This numbness did not become fully complete and is difficult to explain. It felt as though it were deep within the inside of my foot. This numbness radiated outwards from this point and became what felt like thicker with the passage of time. Yet it did seem most grossly unfair, because if you stubbed your toe, you could still feel the pain it caused, because the numbness was deep within.

By the time the numbness appeared I began to visit the local Doctor's Surgery regularly. "Surely they would be able to find out what is wrong and fix it", I thought to myself, but apparently not. My condition continued to get worse. I went every week to no avail. I had every test I could think of and I implored them to think of some too.

Wherever I went, the pins and needles and numbness went too. It all crept up my legs. As soon as the numbness began, the stumbling began and a long line of 'nearly' falling accidents. I could not feel my feet and lower legs properly and consequently, I did not respond to uneven pavements and roads. Work became harder and continued to increase in difficulty with the passage of time. Part of my job at that time, involved visiting people in their own homes and so I would walk in all weathers onto the housing estate. People started to notice my stumbling and were thankfully kind or good-humoured. Unfortunately this did nothing to reassure me.

The numbness continued to creep up my legs and passed my knees without stopping for a break. My hands too began to become numb but thankfully, this happened at a much slower rate. I kept on visiting my GP surgery and made sure I saw more than one Doctor, to increase my chances of finding a solution.

Walking became increasingly difficult. Imagine your legs and feet suddenly stop responding to your subconscious requests to move. Your requests become conscious thoughts and still your legs don't respond properly, because they are no longer truly yours. You have big blocks on the end of your legs, a bit heavier than your actual feet. In order to move, you have to raise a block off the ground using a leg you cannot feel properly. I imagined it was something like being a contestant in the television show from the 1970's "It's A Knockout." Here contestants had to wear costumes larger than they were, including some foam type extra large shoes, which would stick out in front of them. They then had to run and climb over obstacles, reaching the end before their competitors. This was made even more difficult by them having to try and carry a bucket of water, or something similar. The difficulty I faced was frightening and it was no television show. Sadly, it was real life and it was happening to me! This lack of feeling and subsequent difficulty of moving, left me feeling extremely vulnerable. I felt somehow exposed and there seemed to be no one who could help me.

I attended All Saint's Parish Church and at that time was a Christian with a small 'c'. I loved the Lord, yet really only fitted Him into my life to suit me. I had allowed life, busyness and TV to crowd him into the corner He occupied. I did not realise this at the time, yet I know that there are many other people attending Churches up and down the land like this. Despite my small faith, I turned to the Lord for help. My main help then came from the 'House Group' I belonged to. This is a Christian group of approximately 4-8 people who would learn, encourage and grow in faith together. My friends in this group would listen to me talk about my symptoms and then they would pray for me every week. Although there were no answers as such, there was compassion which I needed. I remember catching a cold during this time and being so desperate not to miss the group, I sat with a tissue pressed firmly against my nose all night. I could not sneeze, and no-one caught the cold.

I felt so lost and so alone and yet I was in the midst of people. I continued as best as I could to carry out all my jobs as wife and mother to two gorgeous boys then aged two and four. I did my best at work and in every area of my life, yet it was not enough. So much exhaustion pursued me, as I attempted to carry on as normal. I loved the boys so much and my husband and larger family too. It was so hard to see them concerned for me. It was also difficult explaining to the boys why I could not do something and when I might be able to carry out such an activity. My Husband was concerned about me, and asked what was going to happen next, but I had no answers from anywhere, for anyone.

At that time, I was working 21 hours a week Wednesday to Friday. Each of those days, the boys went to grandparents, childminders or a combination of both. When I left Peter at nursery on Wednesdays, he always cried and I felt bad for leaving him, despite assurances from staff that he soon settled down after I had left. As every working mother knows, this was hard to do and there were times when I wondered if I were doing the right thing. At the end of the working day the rush began in the opposite direction as my husband and I each collected a child often from separate locations. Those three working days for me, were one huge rush. The child-minder, lived just ten minutes-walk from our house. That was a distance I often ran when on my own, in order to get there on time. How on earth would I manage now? I could no longer run!

My body just did not seem to be able to co-operate. I stumbled so much at work and was afraid of what was going to happen next. The Doctor's still had no answers for me, after what felt like an interminable time. I note from my diary that I took two weeks annual leave from work. This began 11th July when the child-minder went on holiday. It made sense for me to stay at home myself to take care of my youngest son, on his usual full day away from myself and family.

Eventually the numbness crept up over my knees into my thighs and headed for my hips. As it progressed my struggling increased. The end of the school term arrived on 25th July. My sister Christine came to visit with her three children. She helped me to get the rooms ready. I struggled and yet I managed and I was glad to have the support of my sister, even though she could not really help with the condition, she helped with physical and emotional support. The boys really enjoyed having their cousins to stay and it was a lovely distraction. We visited play areas and parks. It was so good to see all the children really enjoying themselves, even though I was consumed by pins and needles. I could not stop myself wondering what was happening and what would happen next? It was a very frightening time.

On July 30th I was back at work. I had been to the Crohn's Clinic in Leeds before work. At that time I had the condition Crohn's Disease, which had been diagnosed in the autumn of 1993. This had been a prolonged period for me with much pain and unpleasant tests. At that time, I would awaken a number of nights every week in acute pain as food travelled through inflamed areas of the intestines. I suffered bleeding, but not symptoms so severe that required surgery. There were a number of foods I had to avoid, or face extra pain and Diarrhoea. One such food was sweetcorn and I loved it. Generally my body did not like dense things like pies and many other processed foods. The condition did not stop me from working or carrying out any other job, it just added a further degree of difficulty, especially when I had been awake in the night with the pain. I was often anaemic and felt faint as well as extra tired. I will always be thankful to my husband who would invariably wake up, when I was sat on the side of the bed in severe pain with the Crohn's Disease. He would sit up with me, reassuring me and hugging me until the severe pain past. This was usually 40 minutes to an hour. He made such a positive difference in my life at that time.

This routine appointment at the clinic, was really one of monitoring the condition. I remember struggling to walk across Leeds town centre afterwards, to catch the bus from there to work. My body really did not feel truly my own. I stumbled lots, as I tried to make my legs walk normally. The next day at work, I recorded that I had really struggled to go onto the estate and carry out my visits. I wondered how bad was I going to get? There was no let-up of symptoms.

I managed to host the House group meeting in our home that night. This was easier for me than going out, and I usually enjoyed it. Other people were a positive distraction, yet there was nothing enjoyable about my symptoms and I was really distracted by them.

Saturday arrived and I stayed at home whilst my husband took the boys for the usual day with his parents. My legs struggled to walk and my eyes did not seem quite right. I was exhausted after doing some cleaning so I took an enforced rest.

On Sunday we caught a train to Shipley and walked along the canal to Saltaire. We then caught the train on to Bingley where we visited the 5 Rise Locks. It was a lovely day, yet I found walking so hard. I really struggled and found myself feeling frustrated that my condition was getting in the way. My family were happily enjoying themselves ahead of me and appeared to be oblivious to my struggle. I subsequently found myself complaining under my breath.

On Monday 4th August, I awoke to find my eyes were not seeing correctly. As I looked around the room, everything was going in and out of focus. Not only that, but static solid objects like the wardrobe doors, looked fizzy. As I continued to look around, I tried to focus, yet it was as if solid objects were made up of millions of dots, and these dots were jumping up and down! I knew I needed to see a Doctor immediately. I think my husband must have taken me before he went to work. I saw a Doctor who advised I go to see an Optician that day, so they could take a clearer look. My parents visited that day. They were full of love and concern for me. My father took me to Wakefield to see an Optician, whilst my mother took care of the boys.

I had a full eye test at the Opticians. At the end of this test, the Optician advised me to go immediately to Casualty and she gave me a brief letter with details of her findings. Thankfully, my Father took me to Pinderfield's General Infirmary. His presence was reassuring, even though he did not say much. Once there, we waited to be seen. First, I had to walk down a corridor to a cubicle and climb onto the bed. How I managed that alone I do not know, as my legs were so unwieldy. I was staggering like a child's interpretation of an alien. We were seen by a General Doctor and I was asked many questions. I did not know what some of the questions and answers meant.

I longed for someone to explain to me just what was going on in my body. It was a seething mass of pins and needles by this time. At times, it felt as though they would burst out of my body into the room, as they were so violent! The muscles all hurt too, but I could not describe how? I had never had this sensation before. We had to wait well over an hour for the man from Neurology. "Why Neurology", I thought to myself? I was asked the same questions and more and was then prodded and poked. Somehow, it felt as though I was on trial. Yet what was I on trial for? I was told I needed to be seen at the eye clinic. The appointment was booked for 6th August and I was sent home, as confused as before. My Father was a retired Charge Nurse, but he would offer me no opinions at this time. In hind-sight I am glad of this, as I would not have coped well.

Walking had reached an all-time low. I lost virtually all feeling in my feet and legs. In order to move I had to flick a leg forward from the hip and then put weight onto it. This felt like balancing on a wobbly floor on legs that were not your own. I never knew if a leg would hold me up, as I could not feel it at all! I would look down to see where it was, before I flicked out the other leg from the hip and begin the process again. It felt unreal and unbelievable in one sense. Progress was extremely slow, painful and really hard work. The effort made me sweat, as though I were doing an aerobic physical workout.

On Wednesday 6th August, I should have returned to work, but I was simply not physically able. I believe I had already rung in and spoken with my boss about the situation. He was a kind and compassionate, hard-working man. I do not remember what he said to me, yet I do remember that he was both supportive and understanding, which is exactly what I needed at that time.

That day my Father took me to Clayton Hospital in Wakefield, to the eye clinic. Here I saw an eye consultant. I do not remember having eye drops but I do remember my eyes being examined by more than one person. At the end of this I was asked to wait outside in the waiting area. After a delay, I was called back into the consulting room to be told that I needed to be admitted into Pinderfields Hospital itself. I asked why and when? They did not answer but asked me to ring the ward on a certain telephone number and when there was space, I would be admitted.

"Just what was wrong with me?" I asked myself over and again. I had asked all the medical people I had come across, but no-one had given me any answers. I had no choice but to simply keep going. My parents were very supportive and once I was unable to work they came over twice a week to help me take care of the boys.

Luke was a lovely handful being two years old. I was so thankful he could still go to the child-minders on Friday even though I was no longer at work. At that time, I would stumble about doing my best to do the necessary washing and cleaning jobs required to keep the household ticking over. I had an overwhelming feeling of being trapped in a distorted world of pain, I did not want to be in.

Each week-day I rang Ward 2 at Pinderfield's Hospital. Each day there were no available beds. On Saturday 9th August I simply felt too unwell to leave the house and chose to stay at home whilst my husband took the boys for their usual day with Grandparents. I felt happy to have some peace and quiet. Yet peace was also frightening as there was no escape from fearful thoughts. I had no idea of what was coming next and this truly scared me. I was fighting to make my body take every single step that was required to exist and I felt somehow cheated and angry because of this.

My husband cancelled his Sunday job that week and took the boys out instead, so I was able to rest more. In the afternoon when they returned, I really wanted to enjoy doing something with the boys. As shocking as my condition was, and looked, I managed to stumble and stagger my way to the playground on the estate near where we lived. It is more than unnerving not knowing if you can manage the walk, and not knowing if your body will hold you up and let you walk back again. As a parent you want to give your best to the children and I was determined to do just that. It was scary knowing that I might not be able to come to their aid in the case of an accident. Thankfully there were no such accidents. Looking back, I think my body would have risen to a challenge of any kind, as I know from experience that 'fight or flight' can produce enormous strength.

On Monday 11th August, there were still no beds available on Ward 2. I did not want to go into hospital and yet I really wanted medical help. On 12th August I rang the hospital in the morning and there were no beds again. I felt so alone and I sat at the piano and sang to the Lord. I did not know what was going on. I was not in control at all and I was afraid. Singing and playing basic tunes I had written on the piano, helped me to calm down. As I played, a new song came to me. This was the first song I composed since symptoms started. I called it, "Lamb Upon The Throne." In the song I praise God for His love for me. I knew that He loved me, but I was overwhelmed by the painful symptoms at that time which consumed me. I now know those words were to encourage me, that no matter what goes on in life, God can turn any situation around for good.

Later that same day I received a phone call to let me know that there was now a bed available for me. I was finally admitted on 12th August at 2.00pm. This was an eight-day wait from the start of the eye symptoms, which had persisted. I later learned that this was too long. I did not want to be admitted. The thought of being away from the children was awful. Hospital seemed scary too and I had no idea of what kind of testing would take place. Of course I went as it was so difficult to do any kind of walking and I knew "it" needed to be sorted, whatever "it" was.

2 – Hospital

I was admitted onto Ward 2. This was a 'Nightingale' ward. As you entered the passageway into the Ward there were three rooms on the right hand side, all with closed doors. On the left was a long worktop with office chairs, telephones and a computer and some information binders. As you entered the Ward itself, immediately to your right was the nurses' station. The ward stretched out to the left and the right. The Men's part of the ward was to the left. The Women's side was to the right and looked very bleak from my first impression. The ward was crowded with patients and beds. I was shown to my bed, which was adjacent to the nurses' station. I was left alone sat on my bed, as the nurse who took me to the bed, was immediately called elsewhere on the ward. I was in a ward full of sick people and I felt so desperately alone.

I tried to distract myself from the fear that gripped me, by taking stock of my surroundings. The ward looked dark and dreary as the ceilings were high and there appeared little natural light. There were windows on my side of the ward, but they were too high up to be able to look through and let in little light. The bed I had been allocated, was butted up to the wall of the nurses' station on the left. There was a storage cupboard on wheels by the other side, at the head of the bed. This was modern and large enough to hold a bag of clothes in the bottom, and some books or magazine in the smaller top section. On the top of this unit, later on, came a jug of water and plastic glass. There was just enough room for a plastic visitors chair to fit at the side of the bed, before the next bed took up the next space. The bed also had a table across the bottom of it, on wheels which meant it could be pushed up the bed to suit the user. This pattern was repeated down both sides on the ward on the women's side of the ward.

I did not get very far being distracted as an awful sound began. Sadly, I had to become used to hearing it. It was the cry of distress from a patient. With the passage of time, this would become more than one patient. These cries became louder, the longer time elapsed. Then the cries would turn into moans and then weeping. The nurses came, but it was very apparent that there were insufficient staff, to meet the needs of all the patients.

The moaning and crying from other patients continued and I was forced to listen to their distress, whilst lost in the sea of my own physical and mental pain. I longed for the crying to stop. I waited for quite some time until finally all the cries were answered. The ward eventually became quiet and then the nurse finally came back to me. The pins and needles were consuming me. The pain of the cold numbness in my legs throbbed and I struggled to use the now quite numb, unwieldy blocks called my hands. The nurse began to ask me questions about my medical history and complete the necessary paperwork, before the cries for help began again and she had to leave me once more to answer them.

Eventually, I needed to empty my bladder. The nurse had pointed to the location of the toilets before she left. I stood up, precariously balanced on the legs that truly did not feel like they belonged to me. The Ward floor was hard and marble looking. It looked like it would hurt, were I to fall on it. With every move I made, I did not know if these legs would hold me up. It was really hard work flinging the legs out from the hip in order to balance precariously on each one and move closer to the objective.

I made it and first found two toilets with handrails to help the less able. I did not feel comfortable with using either, as I did not think of myself as disabled. Yet as it was so difficult to move, I used the nearest one of them. The lock on the door was broken, deliberately or by accident I wondered? The toilet was too far from the door to hold onto the door, so I just hoped that no one would burst in. Thankfully no one did. When I came out, I noticed there was an opaque glass window opposite. Although I could not see through it, it let some natural light into what felt like had become my prison.

The exhausting perilous journey back to my bed began, down the middle of the ward. There was no alternative route, so I felt acutely aware of being watched by all the other female patients as I made my way back to the bed. The patients I noticed at that time were all elderly. Some were laid in bed. Others were sat in a high backed chair some had next to their bed. I made it and sat on the bed waiting for whatever was going to happen next. The distressing noises from patients began again and I found it so hard to listen, but I could not block it out. I longed with these patients, that the nurses would come quickly, but waiting seemed obligatory.

The food trolley came for tea and I chose a sandwich. I then struggled to open the packet for some time. My hands could not grip it. It did not occur to me to ask for help to begin with. Then when I looked around, I saw how busy it was and it did not want to interrupt. Neither did I want to draw attention to myself. I remember nearly giving up and thinking it was not worth the stress it was causing me. Yet I was hungry, so I kept picking it up again and again, after having thrust it down. Eventually after many attempts, I eventually succeeded in opening the packet. My heart rejoiced briefly at my success before I realised I had a new problem. How do you get the sandwich out of the packet? Why was it so hard to do? I remember asking myself "How are you supposed to open packets and lift out the sandwich? How do you manage to lift it to your mouth with the partially numb, blockish things called hands?" I was angry, it was almost impossible! It took me some time to achieve, but eventually I was able to eat. I don't remember what was in the sandwich, but I remember bits falling out, as I was unable to hold the sandwich firmly enough. The drinks trolley arrived at some point and I drank some tea and spilled some, as I fought my body to lift the cup to my mouth to drink.

I remained sat on my bed waiting until this nightmare of a day ended. In the evening another nurse came and finished asking the necessary questions and fitted a tag to my wrist. This had my hospital number on it and my allergy to penicillin. The procedure just confirmed my feeling like a prisoner. The evening dragged and was made worse by the two or three patients that had large televisions on the trolleys at the bottom of their bed. They watched endless television, soap operas, chat shows, quiz shows and all sorts of programmes I did not like, or simply just did not want to hear the noise of. I was forced to listen and felt cheated of precious time.

I wondered when the nurses would come and turn off the lights and the televisions? I was utterly exhausted. I struggled but managed to pull the curtains around my bed and get changed into my pyjamas. This was difficult with my hands being so unwieldy and legs so numb and painful, yet I achieved it. It felt like a huge, if painfully slow accomplishment! My heart briefly leaped for joy when the patients had their televisions turned off and the light were switched off! Now I can sleep, I thought to myself. Yet it soon became obvious that this would still be difficult, due to the patients crying out for help. The nurses were just not quiet either, as they walked up and down and spoke to one another. Neither did it feel a safe environment to me. I was in a permanent state of expectancy, wondering what would happen next, in this strange environment. Where was God? I tried to pray over the noise, but I found no peace. After some time and wondering if it would ever happen at all, I did eventually fall asleep.

I had survived to the next day! My legs were still a mass of numbness, pins and needles and throbbing pain. It seemed so unfair that I could not feel them enough to be able to walk properly and yet they hurt so much. It felt somehow as though ice cold water was flowing through my veins. The muscles screamed at me for using them but I made them move as necessary. I was determined I would survive. My hands struggled to assist me in getting out of my pyjamas and into my clothes. I had no intention of staying in bed. Getting up, was of major importance. I was told to go into the 'Day Room', by a member of staff. I had not known there was a day room. It was on the female side of the ward half way down on the opposite side to my bed. When I entered the room, I sighed an internal sigh of relief. The room had large external windows with views of trees and car parking bays. Lots of natural light flooded in, this made me feel there was some hope. There were approximately six tables with four plastic chairs around each one.

Here all the able bodied, male and female patients, came to eat. There was also a television in the furthest corner with high backed chairs in a semi-circle in front of it.

There was a choice of Weetabix or Rice Krispies with milk to eat for breakfast. Alternatively there was toast, which I chose to eat. Then there was tea or coffee to drink. I chose tea, which was served in a pot on each table. I needed to quickly pour it, before it became too strong for me to drink. I did not manage this. I struggled to lift the pot and pour, but I managed some whilst I poured some on the table too. It did not occur to me to ask for help. I was aware there were other patients in the room, but I was largely lost in my sea of pain and did not communicate with anyone.

After breakfast I entered the main part of the ward and saw what a contrast there was due to the lack of natural light. I decided to spend as much time as possible each day in the 'Day Room'. I sat on my bed, as there was no chair next to my bed. A nurse came and told me where the shower was located. I decided not to use it that day, due to the pain I was in and the degree of difficulty involved in getting dressed or undressed. I did go and take a look at it, the next time I went to the ladies toilets. The shower room had a broken lock on the door. That seemed to be a recurring theme on this ward. The plastic shower fitting looked relatively modern. There was some kind of hoist in the room, which took up a large amount of space, but I could see you would still be able to use the shower. There was a plastic chair next to the shower unit. There was no curtain or any type of door so water would inevitably splash about the room. Armed with this knowledge, I planned to return the next morning.

I used the enormous strength required to fling my legs out in turn from each hip and get back to my bed. I waited on my bed, not knowing what for. It turned out to be time for the Consultant's visits. Consultant's and their teams, began the Ward round at 10.00am. I wondered if they would come to me, but they did not. I watched the nurses rush around as the day before. Thankfully there were fewer patients crying out for help in the morning. The tea trolley came at 10.00am and thankfully this was poured for me. I still had great difficulty in lifting the mug to my mouth, but I managed to drink some, with spillages. At some point I was seen by a lady Doctor in a side room at the end of the men's ward. This involved forcing my legs to walk on full display down the middle of the men's half of the ward. I felt really pressurised, as if I were somehow on show. Now I know all the other patients were wondering or guessing what condition I had and feeling sorry for me.

This Doctor was the first really pleasant Doctor I met there. She was very kind and empathetic and her attitude made it so much less stressful. Many of the questions I had to answer seemed the same as asked in Casualty, or by the nurses, but I felt she was really trying to help and was in a position to do something, so I did my best to answer every question as completely as possible. Sadly, she was not able to remove the overriding fear of what was happening to me. Yet she made me feel slightly more hopeful.

Lunch was at 12.00 and served in the 'Day Room' once more. I do not remember what I ate. Yet I remember eating every meal with great determination and gusto. I was very hungry with this condition throughout my stay in hospital, so I fought my body at every meal time to eat. I began to try and talk to other patients that came to the 'Day Room'. I do not remember any of them specifically, just that they had a mixture of physical symptoms and conditions.

In the afternoon a Phlebotomist came and I had a number of tubes of blood taken for some unspecified tests. I asked, but the specific tests that would be carried out were not explained. Once more I was on my own until my Husband and Sons came to visit. I was not prepared for how much it hurt me emotionally to see all of them. How I missed them! I longed to pick up my two boys and hug them, but I could not. My hands would not grip them and I could not pick them up to love them as I wanted. My boys were two and four years old. I just wanted to be with them so much and they obviously wanted to be with me too. I had to stop myself from crying and be cheerful for them. They were as confused as I was about my condition. They asked when I was coming home? I had no answer to give. I felt helpless and cheated and when my Husband asked me the same and more questions, I felt as though he had put me on trial for something, but what? I felt so trapped and tortured by my physical condition and I just wanted to be at home being a mother and a wife. Eventually they left and I could not help myself but shed a few quiet tears. Life was unbelievably bleak.

The pins and needles were flushing up through my back from my waist as well as elsewhere throughout my body. This was unpleasant to say the least. I felt like a time bomb of pins and needles. It was as though they would make my body explode at any given moment. Their impact seemed so great, I felt as though others must surely see this mass of activity going on inside me. It was apparent however, that no one could see. So I was trapped, isolated in this nightmare of pain, where nobody could find me.

My husband returned to visit me in the evening on his own. I missed him and wanted him, but felt somehow suspected of crime by him. Just as he was leaving the leader of my House Group Elizabeth, came with her husband John. It was so good to see them and have what felt like some normality there. They did their best to reassure me and told me that they were praying for me. God seemed so far away from me then. I wondered if He could hear me? I may not have said so at the time, but I was so thankful that they came, as they made such a positive difference at that moment in time. The evening dragged on with the same imposing noises and routine as the previous night. Finally around 10pm once more, the lights were switched off and at some point I managed to ignore the noise and slept.

The following day the 14th August duly arrived. I still struggled to move and yet this had now become normal. It is amazing what we can become accustomed to. I managed with difficulty to get to the shower room and hold on to the shower rail and take a shower. I just hoped no-one would enter and no one did. I was not able to be quick as I found it so difficult. It is hard to carry out specific tasks, when your body does not respond to your instructions. Exhausted afterwards at the amount of exertion taken, I had to lie down on my bed. Whilst I was lying down, I was told by a nurse that I was to be moved to a side room. I had not noticed any such room. It was in the bottom opposite corner to the toilets, behind the 'Day Room'. Staff took my belongings for me so I simply had to force my body to do the kind of stagger, trying to balance walk, down the middle of the ward to the new room.

There were double doors to enter the room, which made it semi-private. What a joy, when the doors were opened. The room contained just three beds and was a room rather than the prison like ward itself. The best thing, were the large windows with the view of the trees and car parks. The natural light streamed in to the room and lifted my spirits. I was given the bed immediately in front of the large window, which of course meant I had the largest amount of light possible. There were two other women in the room, one either side of me with their beds at ninety degree angles to mine, with plenty of room for visitors chairs and each bed had its own high back chair too. What luxury and extra space too. I somehow felt I could breathe more easily.

3 – The Consultant

I was visited in this room by a Consultant, who had a team of students with him. He asked me to take off my sock and with his bunch of keys, scratched along the bottom of my foot. This was more than uncomfortable with my feet constantly throbbing and the violence of the pins and needles raging. He was talking to the students throughout this time and I did not understand the terminology he was using, or the questions he asked the students. He did not talk to me apart from when he asked me to do something. His requests came across as commands and he made me feel increasingly uncomfortable. My knee and elbow joints were tested for reflexes. I do not remember what other tests were carried out. It all seemed strange and confusing. I had no idea what procedures had been decided on at the end of my examination. I realised that I was not thinking quickly enough. This meant that by the time I had questions to ask, the Consultant was long gone.

The next surprise was a Physiotherapist. She had actually come to see another patient in that room. I found myself suddenly asking her if there was anything I could do, to help my physical condition. Surprisingly there were some basic exercises and kindly, she spent a few minutes showing me. I then practiced holding onto the storage unit by my bed and carrying out these exercises repeatedly during each day, in spite of the pain. I decided they could help me to get out of hospital more quickly, so I committed to doing them.

Next I was told that I would be having an MRI scan so that the Consultant could see what was happening in my brain. I did not know when this would happen, or how long it would take? I just hoped it would help with my receiving treatment to end the nightmare I was living in.

I had a pleasant surprise as the Vicar came to visit. This really blessed me. He came outside of visiting hours which of course the dog collar allowed. I went into the Day Room with him. We had the whole room to ourselves and talked about my condition. I do not remember the detail of what was said, but the overwhelming memory is one of encouragement and that I was loved and cared for by God and man.

The MRI scan took place later that day. I was wheeled downstairs by a hospital porter, to the specialised unit. The machine looked huge and very intimidating. The technicians completing the scan explained the procedure. I would be laid on the trolley arm of the MRI scanner, which would retract and go inside the machine. It made loud noises but they would play music to me via headphones, whilst it took images for approximately 30 minutes. I asked if I could have some classical music played. Sadly they informed me there was just some easy listening pop music from the 1980's they would play. I hoped it would not be horrible as I would not be able to take the headphones off, they had explained the need to be absolutely motionless throughout the procedure.

I was taken to a changing room where I changed slowly with difficulty, into the hospital gown. Someone collected me by wheelchair and took me to the machine. What a huge monster it looked. I had to be assisted to lie on my back onto the integrated table, as I was unable to lift my legs and move as needed. Once on, they covered me with a blanket as I was cold. A clip was put on my right index finger, which measured my pulse and I was given an emergency panic button that I could press. It was explained that the procedure could be stopped at any time if I pressed the button. At that point I would be taken out of the machine, but the procedure would have to begin all over again, once I re-entered. I decided that I would indeed remain motionless as instructed and furthermore, I would not panic and have to come in and out. This would be a once and once only procedure. The headphones were placed on me and I did my best to stem the rush of panic, which was trying to overwhelm me. The table I was laid on began retracting into the machine. I was laid on my back and went in head first. They recommended that I shut my eyes. I had by now realised that it was best to listen and follow their instructions closely. I closed my eyes and hoped the time would go by quickly, as I was slowly moved into the machine. It seemed like I was going into a huge washing machine. The technicians spoke to me through the headphones, reassuring me as I went further into the machine. All my body did not go completely in. My feet and legs from below the knees stayed outside, as far as I could tell.

Once inside, I dared to open my eyes after a short space of time. I discovered, when my eyes adjusted, that I was laid in a tube like shape, kind of like a large inner tube of toilet roll. The ceiling of this tube above my head was just a matter of inches away. Perhaps it was as many as six inches. However many inches it was, it made me feel very claustrophobic and I decided it would be better to close my eyes again for the duration of the procedure. I was asked if I was alright and when I said "yes", they told me they would begin playing the music and the procedure would begin. 'Red, red wine' began playing through the headphones. I could cope with that, I thought to myself. Then the noises began. I do not know just how loud they were but I could hear them clearly through the headphones, above the music. They sounded very loud and once again reminded me of a washing machine. It was as if an inappropriate solid item was in a washing machine. This item was flung from one side to the other, as the washer went through its cycle and made loud crashing and banging noises as it went along.

I could not understand why the MRI scanning machine made such loud noises and attempted to block them out of my head, by focusing on the music. This was no easy matter and then another song played which really should not have been in this mixture of songs. 'Do you really want to hurt me?' It was all I could do to keep still! I was a mixture of anxiety due to the scan and a mass of physical pain and the words of this song fuelled my anger. If I could have, I would have given a spectacular verbal explosion! Yet I could not explode, I had to lay still! The song played on and on! I could not move to take the headphones off! I truly fought with myself to stop exploding! This experience felt like one huge endurance test. I spoke to God, but I could not hear his reply, my head was so full of my thoughts. Eventually that song finished, and the music moved onto another hit song from the 1980's. Some songs, I liked and some of them I did not. The person who chose the songs did not choose wisely, but very inappropriately in the case of that particular song. With hindsight, I now laugh at this experience. At the time, I was about as far away from laughter as I could have been.

After what felt like an hour or more and not the thirty-minute procedure that was explained, the banging noises finally stopped. The music stopped playing and a voice told me through the headphones that the procedure had finished. I was desperate to get out! It was such a small space and did not feel like there was enough air left to breathe. I fought with myself to keep still until I was out of this monster machine. It seemed to take more than a few minutes before the table began moving me slowly back out of the machine. The panic was still there, threatening me, until finally my head was out of the machine. I did not plan to go through that procedure ever again!

I was assisted back into the wheelchair and taken back to the changing room. There I found it difficult once more to get dressed. I realised I was utterly exhausted. There was a knock on the door asking me if I were ready, before I was. Everything was so hard! I just wanted to go home, but I could not. Everyone was pleasant to me and yet I was in so much physical and mental pain, I felt angry with everybody.

Once more, I was taken back to the ward by a hospital porter. I remember that I did not have long to dwell on my unpleasant experience as I had visitors during the afternoon and evening from members of my Church including a lady I hardly knew with Rosie and Jim from my House Group. A neighbour came too, which was a lovely surprise.

My husband visited as ever, and I was truly happy to see him. Yet his questions, to which I had no answers, made me feel I was on trial again. I felt as though I were drowning in the symptoms and pain. My visitors could not alter this, as I wanted them to, yet they showed me their love by coming and that held great value.

My brother also visited, which was so good at the time. I have always looked up to him, as have my sisters. I do not remember what we discussed, but he has the gift of being able to find humour in anything and make others laugh. I am sure I will have discussed the MRI scan with him. I remember he made me smile. It was the first time I had smiled in what felt a very long time. Once again, being listened to really helped and the knowledge that he had travelled across from wherever he had been working in Yorkshire that day, to see me. I was hurting, but I was beginning to see that I was loved.

One of the other patients in the side room was discharged and I immediately asked for her bed. That amused the other woman in the room. You see I loved the light, but I did not like the accompanying draught. I have always been a 'cold bod', my mum said and with the MS I felt it more keenly than ever. This was another symptom I did not recognise at the time. Now I had the best of both worlds with a good view with the sunshine and trees, but no direct draught. From this position, through the open door I could see people coming down the ward towards the room. This helped me feel more secure at the time.

I was informed at some point by staff during that day, I would need to have a Lumber Puncture the next day. This was on my mind in the evening. I had heard that they were painful, and this was from everyone. I came from a family of nurses, which was at times useful. This was not one of those times! I had been through the mentally demanding MRI scan that day, and now would have to go through the physically demanding procedure the next day. Would it help at all I wondered? Lots of 'what ifs?' went through my mind. These were always based around what type of illness I had and treatment for that condition. Everything was unknown and I could find no answers. I finally went to sleep.

I had felt cold during the night and yet I was so thankful to be away from the main ward. I still heard many noises, but now there was a door, in between me and them. I still felt insecure on the ward but the side room felt a little safer. I managed yet again with a struggle, to make it to the shower and get washed and dressed. It was such hard work, but it felt so significant to me. Afterwards, I needed to rest and recover.

At breakfast I consciously drank just half a cup of juice as it had been explained to me, the need to lay still for 4-6 hours after the Lumber Puncture. I knew I had an overactive bladder, which could not usually last for that many hours at a time, so I made it a mission to drink nothing else until after the procedure. The day passed slowly, as ever. There were a number of patients who were going to have this same procedure on this ward. At lunch-time, I drank a mouthful of water only, in order to assist digestion. I do not remember what the meal was. I simply wanted my body to digest quickly and remove the remaining fluid before the procedure. My body seemed not to notice how little I had drunk, judging by the amount of difficult walking trips I had to make to the toilets.

Finally between two and three in the afternoon the Doctors carrying out the procedure arrived and all too soon it was my turn. The other patient in the room had left by this time. I had to lay sideways on my bed facing the wall and expose my back for the procedure. A nurse said it should be easy for them to locate the exact location and carry out the procedure quickly, as you could easily see my spine. My ribs and spine have always been prominent, even during the weight gain in pregnancy, so I sincerely hoped the nurse was right.

A Doctor gave me the injection into my back that is supposed to numb the area, but it did not do so. He then pushed in what felt like the width of a knitting needle into my back, to carry out the Lumber puncture. It hurt, feeling as though there was much resistance in my back. He stopped after a short period of time and informed me he would have to begin again. I was waiting for a painful procedure and I just wanted the whole thing to be over! This time it became more painful as he just kept pushing. He kept on pushing and I remember yelling. It felt as though it would go right through me. He finally stopped and then there was quiet before he said, "Oh" in a disappointed tone. I asked him what that meant? He tried to cover up his vocal slip up at first. Then he let me know that although he was now collecting the necessary spinal fluid, it had a little blood in it. He finished the procedure and then left me to stay exactly where I was, as he sought advice from another. My heart sank yet lower as I waited.

There was a delay, of approximately five or ten minutes and then the Doctor returned with someone supposedly proficient in performing Lumber Punctures. This second man informed me that he would have to carry out the procedure again because the sample taken had been contaminated. I wanted to scream, but I managed to contain myself.

I was given another numbing injection that did not work, just like the first. Yet again it seemed grossly unfair that I could feel the whole procedure, when I had almost 100% numbness in my legs and feet, and 95% numbness in my arms and hands. This second man pushed the needle in very quickly and with a great deal of force. I thought he would push me through the wall. I yelled involuntarily and he tried to reassure me, as had the first Doctor. Then quietness and assurance, the fluid was now draining out slowly, and it was just a short amount of time to wait. When you are lying with the pressure of a large blunt knitting needle type foreign object sticking out of your body, which is causing you additional pain when you are already in tremendous pain elsewhere, no amount of time is short! I managed to keep all these angry thoughts inside.

Eventually, the task was completed and the large needle removed from my back. I was assisted either by them or the nurse, to lie flat on my back and then keep still for 4-6 hours. Apparently the longer you lay still, the better. This figure had changed a number of times since it was first mentioned. The shortest I had heard was 2 hours and the longest was 7. As 4 – 6 was the most frequently mentioned I determined that I would get as near to that as possible. I began to get very cold, very quickly after the lumber puncture. My feet already throbbed with the pins and needles and numbness pain and now they throbbed with cold too.

Just as I was wondering what I was going to do my parents arrived.

I was so happy to see them, as I was drowning in my sea of pain. They asked me how I was? I believe I went into precise detail of all the pain and numbness all over my body, and the most recent lumber puncture. My mother sat in a chair nearby, but did not offer eye contact. My Father sat in a chair close to my pillow and chatted after he folded a blanket and wrapped it around my cold feet. He chatted to me about normal everyday life. Part of me wanted him to stop, as I found it hard to hear about everyday life, when I was about as far as you could get from it. Another part of me found it calming. I remember wondering why my mother sat so quietly, not looking directly at me and not saying a word. I warmed up after a while and suddenly became too hot. My Dad unwrapped my feet. I was glad I had been wearing a cardigan for the lumber puncture, as I had found it cold in the room with my back exposed. However, now I was too hot I did not know how I could get it off. My Dad was great, as he rolled me away from him and took the arm nearest him out of the sleeve. Then he rolled me towards him and was able to take the cardigan completely off. Of course, Dad's former nursing skills were great and I was truly thankful. My parents stayed for a long time, approximately three hours or a little more. I will always remember my Father's calming presence and voice at that time. Of course I now know that my mother found it very distressing, to see and hear me, her child suffering so much. She later told me, it was all she could manage, to stay in the room and pray.

After their visit I felt much calmer and wondered how else I could pass the time along, until it was safe to move once more. I did not have long to wait before my next lot of visitors arrived. I had another couple, Mandy and Rupert from the House Group, come to see me. They helped me to keep going. I don't think they enjoyed hearing about the Lumber Puncture. They brought me flowers and I felt loved. It was such a good feeling. They told me that they continued to pray for me. I had no idea what God was doing and found thinking about it or anything difficult, as my head was a crowded mass of thoughts, about the physical pain I was in and the mental distress too. It was good to hear they were praying.

My Husband came to visit on his own without the boys. How I missed the boys! I just yearned to hold them so much. By this time I had laid still for approximately five hours and needed to go to the toilet. Moving was harder than ever and I really struggled to sit up and move to the edge of the bed. I quickly realised that I could not manage to walk on my own, not even to do the painful stagger. I needed his help and so I had to ask for it and spell out exactly what I needed him to do. I put an arm around his shoulder and he held me around the waist. Thankfully in this way, he was able to half walk, half carry me to the toilet. I found myself feeling that I had achieved a great deal, being able to manage to hold onto the contents of my bladder for such a long time. I somehow felt I had made a breakthrough with my husband too. I had asked him for help and he had willingly given it.

My Husband helped me get back to the bed as before, and by this time had begun asking questions again, about the length of my stay in hospital and my recovery. Once more I suddenly felt put on trial. I had no answers to such questions. These were the very questions I wanted answers for myself. Childcare was also difficult. I do not remember where the boys were at the time of this visit. It was apparent that he was finding it hard work being with the boys on his own. I wanted to shout at him. Was he blind? Could he not see that I was in a tremendous amount of pain and could barely move? Yet I did not shout, the anger was quickly replaced with shock as I suddenly saw in my mind the painful creature I had become, in just a few short months. I saw my Husband as part helper, part tormentor. I both loved him dearly and was angry with him. My husband duly went home.

4 – Treatment

A nurse came and informed me that I would be starting steroid treatment. This would not cure whatever was wrong, but would help my body to cope and the symptoms improve. This was the first I remember hearing about treatment. A nurse was already, waiting to put the cannula in the back of my left hand, through which to attach the drip for the treatment to begin. Oh no, I thought to myself as yet more pain ensued as the needle was fitted. Thankfully, the pain was nothing in comparison to the Lumber Puncture. The nurse then fetched a bag of liquid medicine. I was attached via a drip and the bag hung on a stand approximately five feet tall. I asked exactly what the medicine was and she told me I was having 1000mg of Methyl/Prednisolone. As the nurse finished attaching and opened the flow, I saw the liquid starting to come out and into the drip, drop by drop. I had no idea how long this would take but hoped desperately that it would somehow help.

I sat and watched the dripping progress. The nurse later returned to adjust the flowing rate. It took approximately an hour for the bag to empty. A short time after it had emptied, the nurse returned and attached the second bag of liquid, which dripped slowly into my hand. I found the dripping of the liquid strangely interesting and slightly calming too. The cannula was however uncomfortable in my hand and I looked forward to it coming out. Eventually the second bag of liquid was empty and after some delay a nurse came and took the drip and stand away. I expected the nurse to come back and take out the cannula, but no nurse came. I eventually found a nurse to ask for help and was told that someone would get back to me.

Later on, a nurse came and I was informed that the cannula would have to stay in, for the three-day course of treatment. Eh? When had it been decided that I needed this three day treatment, I wondered? I would have to become accustomed to it, I told myself. I got changed even more slowly than usual with the cannula in my hand. Now I already had unwieldy painful blocks on the end of each arm. Added to that, the left one now had a sharp object squeezed into it. Every time I bent my wrist it would sting, as it pricked me on the inside. I tried as best as I could to keep it still. Try as I did, I kept knocking and banging it into me and other objects. How was I supposed to manage? Eventually I explained the difficulty to a nurse who returned and wrapped my hand in bandage, which gave a little protection. I hope I managed to thank her. I could see yet again that this was one busy ward where staff worked really hard. I was later to bed with all that had taken place and I wondered how I could sleep with the cannula in my hand? After a while I did manage to sleep. I kept waking up in the night, each time I moved my left hand and knocked the cannula. Yet I was thankful for the sleep, a brief escape from the living nightmare.

The next day arrived and the degree of difficulty and pain in getting up and moving began again. During the morning I had my second dose of Methyl-Prednisolone and this time I needed to use the toilet so I had to learn how to stagger and move the drip stand as well. I was surprised that it was not as hard as I thought. The hardest part was coordinating everything. I had to move and then get my hands to work to move the stand. The most difficult part was seeing to my clothing when I arrived. Undoing the buttons on my jeans was really awkward. If I could have given myself advice back then, it would have been to wear joggers. Yet I don't know if I would have listened, as the fear of not being able to do up those jeans buttons, kept me wanting to achieve it again and again.

The day eventually passed with my continuing to wonder how much longer would this nightmare last? When would I get better? What was wrong with me? I lived continually terrified and tried my best not to show it, as there was no one who could help me there.

I had four lots of visitors that day. Rosie and Jim came again as did my parents. My husband came bringing the boys. They were very interested in my new room. They were also interested in the cannula, but not wanting to actually see it in detail. How I enjoyed seeing the boys. Yet seeing them hurt as much as ever! I still could not yet hold them and pick them up. The best my body could do was a loose arm around them. They too asked when I would be coming home and that hurt so much. If only I could go with them. I wanted to leave with them so much. Yet I was trapped, caged in this sick body! I thought my heart would break when they left and had to fight so hard to prevent the tears from flowing.

My thoughts were tormented by the pain, all the symptoms and the unanswered questions. We were supposed to have my eldest cousin and partner, come and stay with us this weekend and their visit had to be cancelled. This was the first of many times that things had to be cancelled due to my condition. Thankfully a friend of my husband's whom I had once worked called Jack, came to see me. He brought his mother-in-law too. Once again it was good to feel cared for. We talked about my circumstances and the world outside, which had by now become a completely different way of life, I longed to have back.

It was Sunday 17th August when a new symptom began. My lungs felt as though they were being squeezed. It was as though a giant hand had hold of me, and although I could breathe, I could not do so freely. I could not take in a deep breath without pushing against this squeezing sensation. It was disconcerting and on top of all the other symptoms too. I wondered what would happen next? A Doctor was called and he listened to my chest. I was reassured that everything was normal as far as my chest was concerned. He did not answer my questions about all the symptoms I had. No-one ever answered the questions. It was always the same speech about waiting for the test results. I felt so isolated and desperate. How I longed to go home, and be with the boys and my husband. Yet I knew that things could not continue as they were. The root of the problem had to be found and treated.

I was asked if I would like to attend Chapel? I was not expecting this and was so pleased to be able to say "Yes'". It felt as though a little piece of hope just broke into the prison I was in. Very quickly a wheelchair arrived and I was taken down to the Chapel for a short communion service perhaps 30 minutes long. There were six or eight patients altogether in the Chapel, half in wheelchairs. The Chaplain was very welcoming and gave a short sermon on 'The Prodigal son.' It stayed with me for two reasons. One of them being simply, that it is one of my favourite Bible stories. The second reason was because he gave each of us a bookmark with a picture of a famous painting of the Prodigal son on it. This was a masterpiece by Rembrandt, he explained. I do not remember precisely what he explained, except for one thing. One of the Father's hands in the painting was larger than standard size for that picture. He explained that hand was holding and loving the lost son, welcoming him home, forgiving him in spite of everything. I don't remember his exact words but the image of an ever loving, embracing Father stayed with me.

I had the third course of Methyl-Prednisolone during the day. The day passed and I survived again. Every day it felt like a surprise! I did not record anything else, other than that the chest pain remained. The next day passed uneventfully. I had by now become accustomed to life in the hospital, even though I felt like a caged animal, a mixture of angry and afraid, I had adapted.

On 19th August my symptoms showed definite signs of improvement. My eyesight had improved. I stopped seeing moving dots in front of my eyes. Yet shortly after coming to hospital, as well as seeing the moving dots, my eyes hurt with bright lights. It was as though someone were shining a torch in my face. My husband bought me a number of pairs of sunglasses, until he found a pair that wrapped around and covered my eyes as best as possible. Although my eyesight had improved with the steroid treatment, my sight was nowhere near normal. I could see adequately and yet it was a bit foggy so I could not quite see clearly. The constant need for dark glasses did not help. Yet I did not focus on my eyesight at the time because the pain was all consuming. I hoped it would improve along with other symptoms.

5 - Discharged

I learned I was to be discharged. What did that mean for all my symptoms? What would happen now? Yet I was so relieved that the numbness had begun to recede. It was a very strange sensation as the numbness began to creep down my body, and it was becoming easier to walk. How much better would it get? Would all the symptoms go away? How long would it take? General and vague answers only, were given by hospital Doctors. I was free to leave and so I left the temporary prison that had become a necessary home. I went home without diagnosis and without support of any kind. I was not in a fit state to think about asking for any.

I received a letter from my sister Becky that day, before I left the hospital. She had been praying for me and the Lord had given her a picture of his large right hand. In the palm of His hand I was stood with my husband and sons. The message was "Always remember you are in the hand of God." I felt so lost at this time, so receiving this letter was a great encouragement to me. I did not understand what was happening to me, but surely God must care to give my sister the picture and the message? Yet when would it all end?

I cannot over emphasise just how happy I was to be back at home with the boys. It felt so good to be mum again! The squeezing sensation around my lungs left. What a great relief that was! No longer did I feel I was fighting for breath. I still faced ongoing difficulties each day as the numbness slowly receded little by little down my legs. This meant my walking improved slightly each day, which was great, yet not instant enough for me. Likewise, the numbness in my arms reduced and receded back into my hands until it had almost completely gone. The pins and needles reduced in strength too and no longer felt as though they would explode out of me. They did not leave completely, but there was a vast improvement.

Carrying out the washing remained difficult. I had hoped for a utility room when we moved to our new home. As it did not have one, I insisted the washing machine and tumble dryer lived in the garage. At least it would be quieter, which it was. Now however I saw things in a new light. Getting in and out of the garage was dangerous due to the opening of the heavy sprung door and trying to step inside before it closed on you. Then I had to step down the step onto the garage floor and turn with washing in my hands. I moved as carefully as I possibly could, as I knew the boys could not physically help me if I needed help.

All the usual jobs a mum faces were harder to do, just as they had become before I was admitted into hospital. I was a mixed bag of feelings, so happy to be improving and yet still afraid. I did not know what was wrong with me? I did not know if I would continue to improve until all symptoms were gone? As I did not know what the illness was, I did not know if this had been an isolated incident? I simply had to hope. Yet the "what if's?" nagged at my brain.

I was off sick from work as I was not physically capable of working. I had no idea how long it would be before I was able to return to work? Yet I looked forward to the normality of being there.

My husband was at home on annual leave from work and kept me company during that first week home. I did not ask him for help with the washing and all the household chores. I knew how stressful he had found it, being at home, solely responsible for the boys. I also knew I needed the washing done by a certain time, as I knew all the other jobs that needed to be fitted into each day. A backlog of work had built up in my absence. I think both reasons kept me plodding on alone.

The days passed by and I continued to slowly improve overall. I found it a very stressful time struggling physically with never having questions answered, just waiting for results. Waiting and hoping for the best to come. The overwhelming feeling I was constantly dealing with, was that of feeling alone.

During that first week, I have recorded that my husband took me to Ikea and pushed me around the store in one of the wheelchairs they provided. I hated the fact that I could not walk and needed the wheelchair. I was so angry, but who with? I wanted to go out and yet felt so confined by my body's symptoms when I did. Staying home was no better, as the chores of a mum, were simply harder to do and took longer to achieve. There was nowhere I could escape from the questions in my mind.

At the end of that week, on Saturday 23rd August, my husband and I went out together to a friend's party at their home. A kind neighbour came and took care of the boys. I have no idea how I managed physically or mentally to do that? I do not remember the party. I have just recorded that I went. It will have provided a more pleasant distraction from the constant negative thought life I had at that time. So many questions and no answers filled my mind.

On 23rd August, whilst in what felt like no man's land, the Lord blessed me with another song. This one I called; "Life in Him Completes Me." I do not have many words for this song but simply thank the Lord for what He has given me and acknowledge the fact that I did feel complete with Him. I felt the safest when I sang and played. Yet I could not have told you this at the time. Looking back, I believe God was trying to help me, by encouraging me to spend time with Him. When I sat at the Piano singing and playing, the noise of the unanswered questions in my mind were drowned out. Once more, I did not realise this at that time. I now see how God was trying to get my attention in my sea of pain and get me to cling to him. I felt so far away from God in hospital. Now at home he blessed me through the music, even though I did not really comprehend or understand the power of praising the Lord.

On Sunday 24th August. I started with a sore throat. We went out after the Church Service for lunch with my in-laws. I did not feel at all well, with the sore throat on top of the now milder MS symptoms. Yet I decided that it was better to go, than stay in on my own. Little did I know at this time, but infections would become a constant on-going problem as my body clearly struggled to cope.

The following day the 25th August, my husband was enjoying his second week of Annual Leave. He took the boys and myself to the Yorkshire Sculpture Park. I usually loved it there, but I was frustrated, as I could not walk as much as I would have liked. Everything seemed difficult and so not as enjoyable. Even so, I was glad that I was not on my own with this illness with the boys. The sore throat persisted and squished me some more. I felt truly trampled on by my condition and the world.

During this time of waiting, I would regularly ring my friend Rosie. I rang her every week since I had been discharged. Rosie would listen as I shared all my current symptoms and my fears for the future. I remember going through the possible conditions I might have. The 'what if's' consumed me. I also remember my knowledge of MS was very limited then. Yet what I knew of it, was it being a slow and lingering life suffering until death. That made me say I did not want it to be MS. Even with the little I knew, I was aware that there was no cure. Thankfully Rosie was able to allow me to talk on and on. I would ask what she thought and she was always diplomatic and never really answered. She just let me talk on and on. I am glad she was married, so she would have been able to share with Jim if necessary. I did not notice that God was providing me with what I needed at that time, but he was doing just that. I simply felt so desperate!

At some point during this month, my husband and I were discussing the possible conditions I could have developed. I remember saying I hoped it was a tumour so they could cut it out. My husband was not at all happy with that answer, as he felt it was far too risky and he might lose me! I really had not spent time on contemplating what he was thinking about. I was consumed with me and I realised at that moment that he really cared. Then he made a significant request. He said if I had MS he wanted me to promise to start eating some fish, as it was very good for the brain due to the Omega 3 oils and so on. I had been a vegetarian for sixteen years by this point and so I thought it was a truly disgusting idea! He came up with all the scientific arguments and I could see that he really was trying hard to look after me, as best he could. I did not see how I could possibly eat fish. Then I remembered a conversation I had had with my Consultant after the lumber puncture. At that time, he felt that I had some kind of rare condition, rather than MS. It had been explained to me that MS is a condition that does not have an exact precise test. Instead, it was a lot of ruling out of other medical conditions. The MRI and the lumber puncture were the most accurate tests they could carry out. The longer time went on, the more other conditions were ruled out, so I was encouraged when the Consultant thought it was something rare. All this came to my mind, when I was talking with my husband. I eventually reluctantly agreed that I would eat some fish, honestly believing that this just would not happen.

On Wednesday 27th August I noticed whilst doing the Physiotherapy exercises learned in the hospital, my balance was not as good as in the preceding day. This bothered me, as I had become accustomed to an overall slow but steady improvement in my condition. My parents came to visit that day and were supportive as ever. There was a part of me that wanted them to take control of the situation for me. Yet I knew they could not do so, they were not capable, and I was no longer their daughter at home. I recognised they had no more ability to change my condition than I did.

The following day the other members of the House Group all came to see me and they prayed with me. My balance was a little worse again, so I was thankful for their visit and their prayers. Once more in the midst of suffering, I felt cared for, which helped me to cope.

On Friday my sister Christine visited and took me to a Garden Centre and shopping centre. Whilst I do not remember this occasion specifically, I know she will have helped me to cope. I love Garden Centres, seeing a display of many different plants and flowers in a variety of colours, shapes and sizes. It always gave me a boost to have a visit from a big sister. She has always been very strong and capable and I was happy for her to take charge of me. I have always found it enjoyable to be with family.

The next day, I have recorded that my balance was still not good. I could not help myself but worry about what it meant? What would happen next?

On Sunday 31st August I took the boys to Church and Rosie and Mandy from House Group walked me home. I am sure I will have said "No", to their suggestion of walking me home as I was too proud! Yet I could not exactly stop them. The pushchair, I discovered, was a great walking aid so I achieved the objective. After Church, my husband boys and I, all went as a family to celebrate my mother's 70th birthday with a picnic in a scenic park in Leeds. I was there physically, and yet I was not. My thoughts ran rampant and I found it hard to focus. I remember very little of that time, apart from concern shown for the many plasters on my legs. You see I had really wanted to wear a certain knee length skirt on that occasion and so that meant shaving my legs. That task was unduly difficult! I found myself repeatedly cutting into my leg because I could not feel how hard I was pressing with the razor. Once I started, I was determined to finish the job. Consequently I got to wear the skirt with perhaps as many as a dozen plasters! Unfortunately the activity of the pins and needles had begun to increase. They went from being mild in the background to a strong constant presence in my legs once more, creeping upwards from my feet just as the first time. The numbness began to follow shortly afterwards.

By 1st September I woke to numbness in my right leg that felt almost total. The numbness grew with frightening speed. I did not like what was happening in my body and felt totally helpless to do anything about it. I struggled to keep going, but I would not stop, as I loved being mum to my boys. I was a mixture of confused, lost and yet determined to maintain things.

6 – The Phone Call

Thursday 4th September arrived. It was my eldest son Peter's first day in school. This was a big occasion for both him and myself. He was nervous before we left home, but settled happily on the carpet in the classroom. I am not sure if this were the day I spoke with his teacher or another. She was a lovely young woman who was aware of my deteriorating condition and that it was being investigated. She had wished me well and hoped like myself that it was not MS.

I returned home, I think my youngest went to playgroup as I remember being on my own upstairs in the house. I was sat at my desk when I received the life changing telephone call from my friend Arnold. The call took place around 10.20am. I wondered what could the call be about? I got a big surprise when Arnold told me that God had given him a message during the night to pass on to me. I was a mixture of emotions. Wow! A message from God for me! Yet I wondered why God had not spoken directly to me?

There was no doubt in my mind that it had happened as Arnold was a faith filled man of God, genuine and sincere. I waited with baited breath in anticipation of what the message would be. Arnold explained the message to me which was; "God is going to heal you completely, so don't be afraid. He knows more than any Doctor or any Consultant in the whole World, and He is going to heal you completely." Wow! The message was amazing! Then arose a new set of questions about when and how, to which there were no answers. I felt happy to have received the message and yet confused by it at the same time. Arnold littered his speech with loving phrases, which were great to hear at the time. At the end of the conversation I felt conflicting emotions, knowing I was blessed, whilst having more questions than ever.

I had to leave to collect Luke from Playgroup and return home to make lunch before my parents arrived. I had an appointment with my Consultant that afternoon to discuss my condition. My Father was going to take me to hospital whilst my Mother looked after Luke and collected Peter from school. I focused on moving about the house and completing the necessary tasks. I was thankful of Luke who was a lovely distraction.

My parents arrived after lunch and my father took me to Pinderfields Hospital. I thought I was seeing my Consultant routinely, to discuss my condition. I entered Ward 2 and was directed to the left men's half of the ward, by the nurse. I had to do the stagger/walk down the middle of the ward on full view once more, which was so painful and awkward. As when I had stayed in hospital, I felt extremely conspicuous , as every patient could watch me struggle. At the end of the ward was the side room. I was directed into this room where there were three unoccupied beds. It was a similar to the room I had stayed in on the women's side of ward 2 but it had fewer windows so it was not as bright. I sat on one of the beds and my father sat in the high backed chair next to the bed. There we waited for the Consultant to arrive. When he arrived, he had a group of students around him. I was not expecting that, but everyone has to learn. There were more students than when he had completed the ward round. I do not remember the exact number, but believe there to have been approximately ten students. My Consultant stood at the end of the bed with the students stood behind him and to the side of him.

The Consultant did not approach me but stayed at the end of the bed and informed me that the Lumber

Puncture results had arrived at the hospital. "You have MS" he announced in a matter of fact manner. I was not prepared to hear this devastating news at all! I thought this was a routine appointment? Fear gripped me and immediately I searched for another possibility. "What about the blood tests for the rare conditions you mentioned, have they come back yet?" I asked. "No", he replied. Panic rose in me and before letting him continue, I asked another question about another faint hope I had. I do not remember all I asked, but I remember how desperate I was to hear of another possibility. My heart was racing and I desperately searched my memory for some faint glimmer of hope of another possible outcome. I remembered that at one point, when I had seen him on the ward, he had discussed the possible illnesses I could have. He volunteered at that time, that he thought I had a rare kind of illness, and gave me odds of 70/30 that it was something other than MS. At the time, I was not sure what to believe. Now with the diagnosis of MS I was desperate and just wanted him to tell me it was a mistake. The panic was rising. I wanted him to look again at the paperwork and see a different outcome. No matter what I said, he answered saying I had MS. He said that the Lumber Puncture was 98-99% accurate for MS. I did not want to believe it, it was too much to bear and then he shocked me. He suddenly shouted at me, "You have MS now get on and live with it!" He stormed out of the room. The silence in the room was deafening. Then the students looked at me, looked at one another sheepishly and after a few more moments silently shuffled out the room. I think they were as shocked as I was!

The atmosphere was thick with tension and the shock of those words suddenly descended on me. For a few moments the immense pressure was unbearable. My poor Father had witnessed and heard all that had been said to his daughter. I could not help but think how hard it must be as a parent to hear all that had been said. It was all too much and the weight fell so heavily upon me. My Father managed to say that he was truly sorry I had received such news. The silent tears suddenly began falling down my face. I felt myself slowly crumbling under the weight of it all. Suddenly everything stopped, as I heard Arnold's telephone conversation earlier that morning replaying in my head. I heard his words. They were the words from God. "God knows more than any Doctor or Consultant in the whole world and He is going to heal you completely!" It was a glimmer of hope and it was enough to stop me in my tracks. I was shocked and afraid but I had a small hope. I don't know how long we sat there as time temporarily stood still for me. Then I remember my Father saying that we should leave. He got up and urged me to get up too. I left holding onto his arm and I staggered slowly back to his car in silence. A few silent tears fell from my eyes on the way.

Once in the car my Father again said how sorry he was, and he was so loving, I almost crumbled. But yet again, I began to hear Arnold's words from God play in my head. I found myself being able to tell my dad that I would be healed by God and I gave him the details of God's message from the phone call. It sounded really strange saying it, as though it were someone else and I was listening. Yet it was me, and I knew without a doubt, that strange as it sounded, it was the truth. We sat in silence for the journey.

As soon as I was able to look back on this incident and analyse it dispassionately, I saw that the Consultant wrongly thought I was questioning his ability, in front of his students. I believe he foolishly took my desperate questions, and misinterpreted them as an attack against his diagnostic skills. He obviously had brought issues of his own to the consultation appointment that afternoon.

I found that after seeing my Consultant for some time in the outpatients clinic, he was at first difficult and challenging, but gradually changed for the better. He eventually learned in time to shake my hand when I entered the room and showed some empathy. I believe he must have received disciplinary action which included some training. By the time he stopped being my Consultant, he would give me the warmest welcome possible and seemed genuine. He actually even made me smile. I sometimes wonder whether a student or nurse reported his verbal assault of me? Or perhaps even a male patient who overheard. I am certain that somebody did report him. I am thankful to whoever it was for their part, as I was not capable of taking any action myself. I do not think anyone should be treated as I was, but I believe the Consultant is a better person now. I do not want him to be disciplined further.

Back to 4th September 2003, my father drove me home. When we arrived, the boys rushed to the door, excited to see us again. I felt so shocked and stunned by those words, which ran around my head. We went into the room for a few moments and my mum then followed me into the kitchen. There the force of the news broke me into tears and my mother held me as I cried. I don't remember what she said to me, or what I said to her. Yet I remember she was a lovely mum, there for me to hold onto which I truly needed.

The very next day was Peter's 5th birthday. How do you celebrate when you feel as though you are slowly dying on the inside? Yet the maternal instinct is very strong and so I wanted Peter to enjoy his special day. I put on my cheery face and did everything I could to help him enjoy the start of the day before school.

Sometime after my diagnosis was made known, I began to receive cards from people. They were not exactly "Get Well Soon' cards. They were more of 'Thinking of You.' Most had no words on the front and were simply images of pretty scenery or places. I found these cards very moving and I have kept some. I now think it would have been so much better had I kept them all, but I was not thinking that way at the time. I simply kept the cards that really touched me because of the words people chose to write. Some of the cards were sent by friends in my Church.

Some of the most moving cards were written by people I hardly knew, or did not know at all. My parents attended Harehills Lane Baptist Church at that time, and shared my ill-health with Christian friends. It was some of these friends, unknown to me, who wrote to encourage me; sometimes once, others a number of times over the months ahead. It was so wonderful to think that people I did not even know, cared enough about me to write and encourage me. Most included a Bible verse they had chosen for me. All the cards came filled with compassion and love. I sometimes felt at that time as though I might drown in the stormy sea I was in. Yet these cards were like floating bits of love I could hold onto, like a lifebelt, so hold onto them I did. I remain thankful to every single person who sent me one. I would like to encourage everyone to send a card on any such occasion so that the person receiving them feels loved, in amongst their pain.

On 5th September, my husband took the day off work and he took me to visit Newby Hall and Gardens. I remember not being able to walk as far as I would have liked to enjoy the gardens. The numbness suddenly increased and I wanted to return to the safety of the car. I was thankful to be there, but I felt cheated by the MS and very much afraid of it. As I look back in my diary and other recordings of those days I see how hard my husband tried to be there for me, as best he knew how. At the time I felt he had judged me and found me to be wanting. Now I see he was every bit as confused as I was, wondering what was going to come next. I wonder if it were this day when the topic of 'eating fish' came up. I know it was soon after the diagnosis. I realised with horror that I would have to follow through with that promise I had made. Not only had I been diagnosed with MS, now I had to regularly eat some fish! I could not see how things could get any worse! Everything looked absolutely bleak!

Yet as I look back now it makes me smile, and it has even made me laugh at myself at times. I was so shocked and disgusted with the prospect of eating fish and yet I could not think of a way out of it. I really tried hard, very hard, but there was no opt out clause I could think of. I was going to have to do this truly hideous thing. How could I live with myself? Yet I loved my husband more, and I had given my word to him, which I simply had to keep. I resigned myself to this truly miserable fate!

On 6th September it was Peter's birthday party at a soft play area. This was so hard as I found walking very difficult to do. I looked really off balance and far from normal and I felt as though I were on display again, for all the world to see. I learned that this was the new 'normal' for me. I had to learn to carry on as 'normal' in spite of symptoms and pain. This was now a daily occurrence.

The following day Peter was ill vomiting in the night. My husband saw to him during the first part of the night when I slept so heavily, without any help from medication. I saw to Peter when I heard him cry out later on in the night. I clearly remember thinking on this and many other occasions, "How can I get to him without collapsing or falling over?" Once again the maternal instinct was there and I made it lurching from side to side bouncing off the walls and hanging onto his bunk bed when I arrived. I managed to help him to the bathroom where I sat on the edge of the bath. Thankfully, nearly every time I got up to him over the years he was sick in the bowl or toilet, so I did not often have to try to scrub the carpet. My husband had to scrub the carpet nearly every time he got up. He surprised me, as he did a really good job. He was so good he would often go over the bits of carpet I had occasionally done. He was a great 'hands on' dad. This was, and is, brilliant.

The next day the 8th September, I had an appointment at Clayton Hospital, at the eye clinic. My parents came across and my mother looked after a poorly Peter whilst Luke was at playgroup. My father took me to the hospital. My vision had settled down to a certain degree, following the intravenous steroid treatment. Static objects appeared static again and there were no more jumping dots. Yet the hospital wanted to examine my eyes again. At least they were looking after me, I thought. What I did not realise at the time, was that I could no longer see through my left eye. The length of time I had been left with Optic Neuritis had meant that my Optic Nerve had died. I was told that it was not possible for it to regenerate, the damage was permanent. I was not aware of this additional problem with my eyesight, as it never fully returned to 'normal' so I thought the difficulty was purely the MS. I had light sensitivity all the time, which made me continuously wear dark glasses as everything glared brightly at me and made me feel sick. My husband blessed me, buying a number of pairs of dark glasses, until he found for me the best wrap around pair. I could still see fairly well in spite of the eye problems. To me my eyesight was the least of my problems so I did not give it much attention.

On Tuesday 9th September, my husband took a day's annual leave to help me take care of poorly Peter and Luke. This was proving even harder for me, with the steadily increasing numbness and pins and needles. I did not know how much worse my symptoms would get before they would cease, or if they would cease at all! Looking back in my diary I am blessed to see how much help I received from my husband, my parents, family and friends. At the time I felt truly alone. Yet now I see this was simply not true. At every turn noted in my diary, when I needed help, I can honestly say that God provided it! He did not stop the advancing MS, but I can now see that He was there with me. The trouble at that time was that my head was crowded full of negative thoughts, so I could not hear Him, or feel His presence.

On Wednesday 10th September Leeds City Council held a Conference for disabled employees in the Civic Hall. I had such conflicting emotions about the whole event. I felt so pleased that the Council were holding this event, and that I had been invited. This was due to my informing them I had 'Crohn's disease'. I really wanted to attend and to be with other disabled people. Did that mean I was truly disabled? I had been able to work along with everyone else even after these new symptoms started in May. I had kept working until I could no longer walk in August. I did not see myself as really 'Disabled'. Surely I would get better and go back to work? Surely everything could be as it was before? I did not want to be disabled. I wanted to attend yet how could I, when I had such difficulty walking?

Well I did manage to attend, with all my conflicting thoughts and emotions. My husband dropped me in Leeds on his way to work. I do not remember anything that was discussed. Yet the overwhelming memory was one of the mixture of people with different disabilities, some major, some minor. One of the speakers was in an electric wheelchair and whatever her difficulties, she had overcome them and achieved much in spite of them. I am thankful to Leeds City Council for hosting this event and inviting me. Even in my confused and mixed up state of mind, it helped me to see that there were possibilities for a working life at some point in the future.

Another day, I am not sure which, I took Peter to school and saw his teacher. She asked if there had been news and when I told her I had been diagnosed with MS, she jumped out of her chair and rushed over to me, giving me the biggest hug. I was broken, but she demonstrated her love, which reduced me to tears. I fought back the tears for Peter's sake. I did not understand what was happening to me? When would it end?

My symptoms continued to deteriorate and won the battle for supremacy in my body. The strength of the pins and needles increased daily and the numbness followed suit and threatened to swallow me up. Not only that but I recorded on 11th September that I was finding it difficult to release the muscles in the bladder in order to wee. I had thought in detail about this process only a couple of times in life, like after childbirth, when the bladder took some days to fully recover before returning to normal function. Yet here I was, having to think about what my body was doing and try to release those muscles to perform this basic but vital function.

By 12th September my left leg was almost completely numb once more and I noted, I had another sore throat. Sore throats, colds and other common ailments became constant regular companions for years. On 13th September Peter went to stay with my sister Becky. It was so good to have family relatively close by. Peter loved his cousins and was overjoyed to stay the night with them. This meant that I would get a good night's sleep. When my husband left early the next morning for his Sunday job, I could stay in bed resting that little while longer until Luke was up. I do not believe I went to Church, as I could not walk well enough by that time. In the afternoon we went to my niece's birthday party, where Peter had been thoroughly enjoying himself. I was so glad to have help and yet I wanted to escape.

By 14th September the numbness increased greatly in my hands. It was almost complete in my left hand and also just slightly less in my right. This increased the difficulty of completing everyday tasks. I felt as though I was on a rollercoaster ride I did not want to be on. It was running away and frightening me and I just wanted to get off. Unlike a rollercoaster, this was not just for fun, it was real life, and there was no choice but to continue.

On15th September the numbness had reached up from my legs past my hips and now reached my waist. I remember wondering as I did before, with this degree of numbness, how much longer did I have left before it was total? It was as though a big part of me was no longer there, just like the 'Invisible Man' I thought. Only it wasn't, because he could easily walk about!

On 16th September my menstrual cycle began. The increased numbness in my fingers made coping with this really difficult. I was already struggling and found myself wondering how are you supposed to open packets of sanitary towels and tampons when you can no longer properly grasp and hold on to items? Trying to open any packaging when it feels like you have thick padding on the end of each arm instead of a hand is a nightmare! Well I found you just have to keep on trying, until you succeed. Of course it meant that things got dropped and were wasted. Yet I found that I was not prepared to give in. Today I would look to see if there were an easier solution to the problem. Back then I was angry with the world, and so stuck at whatever it was, until I achieved the objective. At the time it seemed so frightening, because I struggled so much to perform every day functions, and I feared that being able to do them was about to disappear completely.

On Wednesday 16th another mum, Alice, brought Peter home for me. This was the first time I recorded such help. I was blessed to have made friends with this mum who lived in a nearby street. She had a daughter in the same class as Peter, and was willing to listen to me and be as supportive as she could be. I did not feel able to share everything with her as I hardly knew her, yet she provided me with the help I needed. Thankfully, Peter was an understanding, well behaved child. He was happy to help me by coming home with another mum, as my legs would no longer get me to the school and home again. Alice helped me on many such occasions and it made a positive difference every time.

7 –Admitted Again

On 18th September I saw my Consultant at the clinic on Ward 2 and he admitted me to Pinderfield's Hospital once more. I attended with my bag already packed, as I suspected I would be admitted when he saw me. I did not want to be in hospital, and yet I realised, this was where I was most likely to receive help. I did not know how I would cope. I remember saying this to my mother, prior to the consultation. She went away and prayed and came back to me saying that God had assured her He would go with me. I did not hear from God like that and wondered what on earth that was like? Yet I believed completely that she had heard from the Lord. So God would go with me and He was going to heal me completely at some point too. This helped me cope a little better.

The following afternoon, I should have had a visit from Personnel, at home. This was cancelled, which at the time I found a relief. I felt under great pressure to say when I would be back at work, and yet I had no idea when that would be? I was not questioned extensively by my employer at all! Yet I knew it was standard procedure to give an estimated return to work date. How could I estimate when I could walk properly again? I wanted to know the answer myself, but there seemed no one able to give such answers. I had kept sending in Doctor's sick leave notes and had to continue in this way for a long time. The sick notes given by my GP at that time were for two weeks duration. That same Friday, I began a three-day treatment of Methyl-Prednisolone at 1000mg per day, as previously.

Hospital still seemed as scary a prison as ever. I was helped initially by being placed in a side room on the right hand side before entering the ward proper. This small room had its own window with obscured glass. It also had its own sink and most importantly its own television! Although I felt caged, at least I had some comfort. I believe I had two nights here until a new mum needed the room. This lady had given birth to twins and suffered some neurological problem during delivery. I was asked to move from the room by the nurses because her new-born babies could not be brought onto the main part of the ward. Though I was disappointed to move, I felt the anxiety for her, of being separated from those babies and so of course I immediately agreed. I remember her later thanking me for making it possible for her husband to bring the babies to visit her whilst she was a patient on Ward 2.

Whilst I was in this private room, I was visited by a good friend from work. She came with her partner and managed to make me laugh! This was so good and I really enjoyed her visit. Sadly, she later told me she was not able to handle seeing me in this condition and did not return. In hind-sight I am glad she came as her visit had a positive impact. I was upset that she did not keep in contact after this time, but it was good that she was honest with me. At least there were no 'what if's'.

I was moved to the same side room at the bottom of the ward as last time. There was just one patient in this room at that time. This meant I was able to choose to have the bed next to the window or wall, the one with the view of the ward when the doors were opened. I chose the latter, as I found some security in being able to see someone approaching the room. Now as I look back, I see God's hand in operation, seeing I got a private room to start with, then the next best thing, giving me the room with the most sunshine and view. This gave me a small sense of some security, in the midst of the terror of MS which had thrust itself upon me.

Eating and drinking was truly problematic. At breakfast I chose to eat toast, the easiest option. Yet picking up a knife and spreading on the margarine and marmalade was really difficult. The knife would not stay in my right hand and my left was even worse. I found with persistent effort I would eventually get some marmalade on the toast. Then there was the struggle to pick up each piece, and hold onto it, until I could take a bite, chew and swallow. Once I had managed this then I had to laboriously repeat and repeat this process until I finished. It would have been far easier not to bother with eating, but I had a ferocious appetite with the MS attack, just as last time and my internal anger fuelled my desire to eat. Drinking was almost impossible. Pouring the tea from the pot was ridiculously hard and after spilling liberally across the table, I finally accepted help. That was offered gingerly by other patients who I think read my anger. At every meal I faced the same difficulties of not being able to retain hold of the cutlery and repeatedly dropping them. Yet every meal I finished in order to satisfy my hunger. My eating will not have looked pretty. Gravy and sauces were inevitably splashed about, but I survived as did the other patients.

Saturday 20th September, I had my second day of Methyl Prednisolone. Unlike my first stay in hospital, this time I really looked at the other patients and tried to be sociable. After all, they were unlikely to be happy either, being in hospital for whatever the reason. Then I found it hard, as I was asked what condition I had? I had to say MS and I did not feel ready. It all seemed too soon. It had only been a matter of four months from the first symptoms to the state I was in now! What was going on? I just wanted to leave but I was trapped in a foreign body. I could not manage to walk convincingly, never mind walk off the ward!

I noticed a patient, a pensioner called June. She was in the bed closest to the ladies toilets and shower room, so I went past her bed frequently. She soon spoke to me and I had to respond to her. You see, she spoke in kindness and I could not respond with the frustration and anger I felt on the inside of me. June was frail and like me she was afraid. I recognised that, and we soon became allies in the prison we shared. We would talk at various times each day and she was overjoyed when Peter and Luke came to visit me. They were shy of June at first, but gradually learned to trust the sweet pensioner she was.

There was a male patient I will call David. He was one of the few able bodied who came to the dining room/lounge. He was a 'happy -chappy.' At first I wanted to keep him at arms-length as I did with others. I soon learned though, that it was good to be around him. He seemed genuinely happy, in spite of his medical condition. He was constantly seeing humour around him and laughed regularly. He reminded me of my brother and I found myself wanting to hear his jokes and laughter.

Also admitted onto the main part of the ward during my second stay, was a bedridden woman who looked to be in her forties. I would find my eyes drifting across to her. She had her arms in some kind of splints. The ends of her fingers bent over each arm piece. I was horrified when I learned she had MS! She was not able to move, but lay still all day and night in bed. I occasionally I saw her start to raise an arm, but that was all. Did having MS mean I would end up like that? Unable to do anything, but lay there? I had been told I had Relapsing Remitting Multiple Sclerosis, but that meant nothing to me. I had also been informed there were other kinds of MS, so I hoped this poor woman's type was different to mine. It was still frightening, whichever way you looked at it.

In the side room I was in, was a patient called Mary. She was the only patient originally in that room. Her bed lay in the position with its head back nearest to the door. I do not remember her condition. Yet I remember her telling me that she could not sleep. She stated that she never slept. Mary would watch television for some time after I announced that I was going to sleep and switch my light out. I had to try not to be agitated at the TV noise. At least in the side room the moaning and other noises of the ward were dampened down. I found it hard as I lay there trying to ignore the noises and pain I was in too. It was like some kind of endurance test. Only I had no idea of when the test would end? I wondered numerous times in hospital how would I get to sleep? I am the type of person who needs peace and quiet to sleep so this was difficult anyway. Yet I did eventually sleep and awoke each morning to hear Mary snoring away as she slept!

I don't remember if it was the same day or the next until a new patient was admitted into our corner bay. There were now three of us and then a fourth bed was squeezed in. The newest patient Molly, was loud and inconsiderate, I thought. She wanted to talk lots and I felt she was an intrusion. I did my best to stay clear of her, as I could not answer her questions about the MS and did not want to think of all the possibilities that arose from her questioning. I also found I did not want to share about my home life. Somehow, I wanted to protect it, as if it was under threat.

Molly continued to ask questions and talk to me more than the other three women in the room. Why does she want to talk to me? I thought. I remember one morning struggling to walk and leave the room to go and have a shower. My arms were full with the towel and my toiletries and trying to balance with my arms. Both the two other women offered to help me. I must have looked terrible flinging those legs out from the hips and trying to balance on them. I did not want help at that stage, because I was too proud and determined to achieve the objective. Accepting help, meant that I acknowledged I could not survive on my own. I made things much harder for myself. As I look back, I can see that it would have been so much better to accept help, every time it was offered.

On this particular morning, I headed with great difficulty to the shower. On top of the other two women offering help, Molly began speaking to me. I have no idea what she said. I just remember that it was too much for me to cope with so I kept going as quickly as I was able. I reached the shower to discover for the first time in hospital, that someone else was in it! I could not face the painful walk back to the side room. I most certainly did not feel capable of facing Molly. Then I noticed a plastic chair had been placed near the shower so I sat down and waited for the thirty minutes it took this woman to have her shower. I squished my agitation when I realised I was not going out anywhere and the woman in the shower must be in need, as I was. I am so glad I did not give in to bang on the door. When the door finally opened, I saw it was the mother of the newly born twins. She told me how much she enjoyed being able to have her first shower since giving birth. Seeing the joy on her face meant I broke into a smile. It was worth waiting for that.

After my shower I felt a little better as though I had struggled, I managed to achieve the objective. I slowly made my painful stagger back to the side room. Here I found the other two women in the room talking with Molly who burst into tears as I entered the room. Suddenly, I was filled with compassion for Molly. I sat on the bed next to her and put my arm around her. I discovered, as she cried and talked that she had MS too. This was why she had wanted to talk with me more than the others. She had some family relationship problems too and I found myself listening and trying to point out the positives from what she had told me. After some time, she calmed down and then went for a shower herself. I felt so bad that I had previously tried to escape this woman, who was obviously in need. I did not feel qualified to help her and felt I had not known what to say. I could have made things worse? Yet as I look back today, I see that Molly simply needed to be heard and showed compassion. I don't think my actual words really mattered.

The two women in the room then astounded me. They declared how glad they were that I had gone and helped Molly, as they had not known what to do? I did not feel I warranted any praise, as I had effectively run away from Molly earlier on. I hoped someone better qualified, a family member, or someone else, would come to take care of Molly. I did not feel up to it and I did not desire to do it either!

On Saturday20th September I had another dose of Methyl-Prednisolone, 1000mg as before. I was blessed with visitors that day. My sister-in-law came with her two children. The children were a lovely distraction, but the questions asked were the same ones that I could not answer. I found it hard not to be frustrated. I was blessed with more visitors. I am so glad that people came, as it helped to relieve the tension. My husband came with the boys. That was always the hardest one. I just felt the strongest desire as mum, to go home and simply enjoy being mum, but I could not!

My sister Becky came, which was really good. We had been quite normal children growing up, mostly playing well together, but often fighting with each other too. She was older and bigger than me and always won when we physically fought, until I finally realised I could bite! She stopped winning every fight after that. Once older, we had become great friends and so she became a great encourager to me. Becky brought her daughter to visit too. We have always got on famously, so once again it proved a great distraction for me. My husband returned to see me later on his own. As I look back now I can see he really loved me. In his own way he was simply confused and stressed with what was happening to me.

On Sunday 21st I awoke with chest pains. It was that same lung squeezing sensation again. I was not happy to feel its return on top of the huge amount of other symptoms. There seemed to be not one single area in my body that was unaffected! I wanted to shout and scream, but what? And who would I shout at? The pins and needles threatened to consume me day after day. I wondered how much more pain I could endure?

I had my third day of Methyl-Prednisolone in the morning. Whilst I was hooked up to the stand, the volunteers arrived to take me to Chapel. I suddenly thought I would not be allowed to go and this made me sad. I realised how much I enjoyed turning my attention to God. Thankfully, I was still able to go and the volunteer pushed me in a hospital wheelchair, whilst I held onto the stand as the steroids continued to drip into my arm. It was a traditional Anglican Communion service of which Christ's suffering on the cross took on extra significance. I looked around at the others present. All bar one of the eight that attended, were in wheelchairs.

It was so good to have escaped the ward. I realised for the first time, when I was taken back to the ward, I was not consumed with terror. I realised for the first time that God really was there with me, just as my mum had said. Perhaps He was listening to all my desperate 'help me' prayers. I did not understand what He was doing or what He wasn't. Recognising He was there amongst all the pain helped, even if I could not hear Him or feel His presence.

Late morning brought Sheila, who was my closest friend at that time. I knew Sheila from when we both lived in Leeds. Now she lived in Newcastle with her partner and their young child who came too. She was shocked as I was, but she provided strength and normality that I needed. My husband arrived and I was able to leave the hospital for a few hours. We all went out and had a pub lunch. That was so strange. I could only just walk and I was in so much pain. Yet here I was sat in a pub trying to make my fingers use cutlery and retain hold of a knife and fork, in order to cut food up into bite size portions. Sheila seeing me struggle, stepped in and chopped up my food, as she did for her child. I longed for my husband to have seen I needed this help. I longed for someone to take charge of all of the daily difficulties of the MS. I felt so lost and alone in amongst people and I did not know what would happen next? It was a very painful time emotionally.

I remember talking with Sheila in the hospital café. I do not think it was the same day. On this particular day, the shocking nature of life being snatched away from me, suddenly hit home. I broke down and cried properly for the first time since this whole chapter of my life had begun, just four months ago. I did not realise this had been the case, until that moment. Sheila was great. She listened and gave physical and emotional support. Her partner Sam was great too keeping the little one entertained as I swung from sobbing uncontrollably to talking things through with Sheila. She really met a need I had not been aware I had, until that time. I had spent a lot of time and energy on not crying in front of the boys and my husband, as well as friends and family. I will always be really thankful for her and Sam's invaluable support at that time.

Later on that day Rosie and Jim came to visit me once more. I was glad to see them both as they brought a level of normality to me. I had realised by this stage that I had a real need for people. They were not able to answer my questions any more than the Consultant's, or any medical staff. Yet they were able to show me love by visiting me. I did wonder if I would be able to cope and stay sane much longer, but I believe all my visitors helped me to do exactly that.

Now it was Monday 22nd September and I was blessed with many visitors that day, including my Consultant. He had decided to start me on a slow reducing dose of steroids to continue once I left hospital. He felt this would give my body longer to recover. I started with taking 40 mg of Prednisolone that day. I really did not understand what was going on. I knew that the steroids did not cure the MS, but kind of caused it to freeze and stop where it was. Yet what did cure MS? When would I recover and when could I go back to my life? These and many other such questions flooded my mind constantly. I wanted to get back home and return to my normal life as soon as possible so I was happy to take this reducing dose. I felt so far removed from my normal life, so it was good that I began to show the first signs of improvement in my walking that day. I was relieved to see my body start to respond to the treatment. Yet fear still gripped me, as I did not know what frightening thing would happen next?

During that same day, I was visited by an Occupational Therapist. It had been decided that they would make an assessment of my home to see how well I managed and what aids and adaptations I could benefit from. Just four months ago, I had visited elderly tenants to assess their needs, as part of my job. I ordered external grab rails, bath rails and lever taps to help them manage in their homes. Now here I was, needing a similar visit to assess my needs. It seemed so unfair, and yet I could see it was necessary. I was glad I would be receiving some support, and not left to just struggle on my own, as it had seemed last time, yet at the same time, I did not want help!

I have recorded that my parents took care of Peter and Luke during part of the day. This meant my husband was able to visit me on his own. Once again I was so happy to see him. Yet this happiness would melt away when he began asking me questions. I did not know how long I would be in hospital, or when I could go back to work? Neither did I know who could help with the children? I realise in hind-sight, how isolated he felt too, and how he had no one to share with at that time. In hospital though, I just felt like one big ball of pain. I just wanted him to come and rescue me. Yet of course, he could not do so!

A Physiotherapist came to see me on Tuesday. She gave me exercises to do to help improve my walking. She came each day to see how I was progressing after that. As I wanted to go home as soon as possible, I worked hard at the exercises. On this visit I was shocked and dismayed to see that she had brought with her a walking stick for me. I was thirty three years old! I did not want a walking stick! I did not think I needed one either! The Physiotherapist had other ideas. I objected vehemently with every argument I could think of. The Physiotherapist asked me to try it as she felt it would help me balance and walk better. I had to walk down the middle of the ward with at least one nurse, other staff and patients observing. I was so disappointed to see that it did help me balance. I hated it with a passion, yet she and other nurses commented on how much my walking improved, as a result of using the stick. As much as I did not want to, I took the stick!

This of course fuelled my anger, but I was rescued when I had two visitors from my Church family that day This helped me to calm down and stay sane through another extremely stressful day.

On Wednesday I saw the Physiotherapist again. I had an assessment on the stairs, to see how I coped. I tried so hard to manage perfectly well, I was so eager to go home. I believe it was that same morning the Occupational Therapist and her student, took me home to assess my needs in the house. That was so strange, having people take you to your own home, to observe how you managed. I suddenly saw the house through medical eyes. The need for hand-rails in the shower was found. One was also needed, adjacent to the downstairs toilet and in the en-suite. A hand-rail was also ordered near the front door, for me to hold onto as I unlooked the door. This felt so hard, as it felt as though I was advertising to the world, now I had MS and was disabled. I did not feel ready! And yet I could see that I needed help, and all that the Occupational Therapist said was true. I found it shocking, once again I felt it had been thrust upon me, without any choice in the matter. It was my body, and yet it felt like someone else's.

Back in hospital I was visited by a good friend I had travelled abroad with some years earlier. Cathryn was visibly shocked to see me in such a condition. She asked me lots of questions, as everyone else. By now I had learned to give answers that caused me the least amount of mental pain. She brought me a large beautiful bouquet of flowers. I felt so touched by her kindness in such a generous gesture. Yet the shock I had seen on her face made me wonder if she would return? I felt I had become some kind of alien being, and I just wanted to escape – but how could I?

My condition continued to improve steadily following the three days treatment of Methyl-Prednisolone. Each day brought slightly more feelings back to my hands and legs. The tightness in my chest left, as last time, and it was a relief to see my body in the recovery process once more.

Pam visited me again, always full of smiles. I found myself drawn to her. She was full of joy all the time and I wanted that. How could I possibly be full of joy when I was overflowing with pain? What was God doing? Was He doing anything? I was so full of fear, I was unable to see out of that box. Now as I look back, I see He was providing me with the support I needed. He was there all the time, but I could not hear Him, or see His hand at work as my head was crammed full with negative thinking, fear and anger. This meant I felt really mixed up about God. On the one hand I felt so alone, on the other I knew God must be planning to heal me as I had received the phone call from Arnold. There was no doubt about his sincerity. I knew it was the truth. It was simply so difficult to think with any kind of clarity, my head was so overcrowded!

Mandy visited too that day, as did my sister-in-law later on. It was good to see them. They both told me about things that were happening in their lives. I enjoyed hearing about family life and once more, desperately wanted my family life back.

8 – The Vision

Unbeknown to me, on Monday 22nd September, in the evening, there had been a prayer meeting in Church for me! I heard of this, from the Vicar's wife later that week. At this meeting when they had prayed for me, a lady in the congregation received a vision. In this vision, the lady saw a tree. A gardener came along and began digging around the tree and cut through about half of the tree roots. The roots were left uncovered and exposed. The buds and leaves on the tree shrivelled up and the tree looked as though it might die. As she continued to watch, new roots grew out from the tree. These grew much wider and deeper than ever before and anchored the tree more strongly. Then new leaves opened up and the shrivelled buds opened up into the most beautiful blossom.

A word of knowledge was given about this vision. Apparently, I was the tree in it. The damaged roots were the nerves in my body with the damaged myelin sheath, that usually protects them. The new roots growing represented my faith growing, with me tapping into other resources that would build me up, stronger than ever before.

When I heard this, I was as ever, a mixed bag of emotions. I was pleased people had prayed for me. I was happy God had sent a vision. I was unhappy that I was depicted as the tree, for I knew that trees do not recover quickly, but take years to recover. I did not want to do that. The letter the Vicar's wife sent to me, explaining all of this, was filled with compassion and the love of the Lord. I could not really see that when I read it at that time. Yet it still gave me hope, as confused and mixed up as I was. I would read and re-read the letter time and again, as I could see there was hope on the pages, even though I could not precisely point to it. When I read the letter before I wrote this chapter, what joy filled my heart! I felt the love of the Lord for me through those words and it was so good. I will always be thankful for the love shown to me by the vicar and his wife. I am also thankful for the love from all of my Church family. What a positive difference they all made! In hospital, they really helped me to cope with the very frightening situation I found myself in. This was true of all my family and friends too, who provided a lifeline for me to cling to.

On Friday 26th September I was reduced to 30 mg of Prednisolone a day and given instructions on how to take the rest of the course. I could now safely lift a cup of tea to my mouth. I still spilt at times, but at least I could now hold the cup more securely and drink better, an improvement since admission.

Later the same day I was discharged. What a relief to be able to return home! I was happily reunited with the boys. I remained so uncertain about what the future held for me, but at least I was home. The struggle began again as I took on the physical tasks associated with being a mother and housewife in this awkward, painful mass, that was my body.

The very next day, Saturday 27th September, Peter had a birthday party to attend. I have to say at this point that I don't know how I had somehow signed up to be the parent that always stayed with each child at birthday parties. This was the pattern that remained throughout the boy's childhood.

At this party, I began to discover some of the difficulties faced by disabled people. The party was held in a family pub, which had a children's soft play area. I was going stay with Peter whilst my husband went to buy the weekly shopping with Luke. At the family pub I was directed to the rear entrance, to the door that led straight into the soft play area. The first problem I faced was that the rear of the premises was on a downward sometimes uneven tarmac slope. I was struggling to walk as it was, so this slope proved difficult, especially when it got steep. When I made it to the door, there was a threshold to step over. When you step up and across something as in this case, you really have to balance. I struggled to do it and longed for the premises to have proper level access. I made it through those challenges and onto the next.

The room was full and noisy, with chatting adults and shouting, happy children, who were just out of sight in the play area. There were perhaps eight low tables with small chairs around them. The adults had pushed some of these chairs and tables together to sit in groups. As I quickly looked around, I did not recognise anyone. There was no one to greet me when I entered. I looked for somewhere to sit and realised how this objective would not be easy to achieve as everything had been made with children in mind. I saw at the far end of the room was a flight of stairs. Next to this was a lone chair. Peter could not see his friends and was a little nervous in the new environment. Hoping I would not fall, I struggled across the room and made it to the chair and managed to sit down without falling. That was a massive achievement, which nobody realised.

I encouraged Peter to take off his shoes and go and play pointing him in the right direction, hoping he would see his school friends quickly to reassure him. He must have done so, as he did not come back. I was then sat there with Peter's shoes and coat and had to take my own coat off as it was warm in there. Putting on and taking clothes off is not easy to do when you have reduced feelings in your arms and hands. In hospital I had managed to pull the curtains around my bed to get changed. I felt truly a public spectacle, as I tried and kept trying to take my coat off. First I struggled to undo the zip. My hands would not grasp the zipper and hold on to it. I was beginning to think I would melt as I got hotter and hotter. I was tempted to give up trying, but the heat kept me going. I remember muttering lots of "stupid" under my breath.

The mum, who was hosting the party then appeared and welcomed me. I needed help, but I could not bring myself to ask. I did not want to ask, I wanted to manage. I also did not want to admit that I could not manage. I feel sorry for that person as I look back at the emotionally knotted, mental condition I was in. The host was quickly called away and I was left alone once more. I don't know if I had managed to get my coat off by then but eventually my fingers managed to successfully deal with the zip and I was able to take the coat off. It felt as though it had taken a really excessive amount of time and energy to achieve. My struggle was so public and I did not know if anyone cared, and somehow that mattered to me.

Peter suddenly returned needing the toilet. On one wall of the play area were the children's toilets. The first challenge was standing up after having been on such a low chair. I wondered how anyone with a physical disability could manage? I said lots more "stupid" under my breath. Eg. "Stupid chair, stupid table, play area" etc.) Peter was oblivious to my struggle, which was for the best. I had difficulty in using the door handle into the toilets to start with. Once I managed to finally open the door, I found three small children's toilets. Obviously these were ideal for the children but not for the adults I. I wondered where the adult toilets were? When Peter had finished we tried to leave the cubicle, but I could not turn the knob that locked us in. My fingers would not grasp once more.

Peter became anxious when it became obvious I could not open the door. He tried and could not manage it either, I do not know why? It seemed a ridiculous situation to be in. I did not want to have to explain to anyone, how or why we were stuck. I managed to calm Peter and myself, explaining that nothing would happen to us as we waited safely, until I managed to open the door. Eventually, as with the zip, my fingers obliged and turned the door handle. We headed for the low sinks where I found taps difficult to grasp to use. I said lots more "stupid", under my breath. I eventually achieved the objective before the last trial of opening the final door to re-enter the play-room. It was easier this time and we headed straight for the chair where our coats waited. Peter unceremoniously flung off his shoes and ran back to play. I managed to balance on my legs and sit down safely again. I was left wondering how many more challenges lay ahead. Was this what life was like for disabled people all the time?

I looked with fresh eyes at the premises. There was nothing cute about the children sized tables, chairs and toilets. They were totally impractical for me, and anyone with a physical disability. The room seemed hotter than ever, and I wanted a drink. On two of the tables, stood large plastic jugs of orange and blackcurrant squash. There were about a dozen children's plastic cups with each. I searched the room with my eyes for a vending machine for adults but there was none. I did not want to drink the children's juice, as it was obviously meant for them and not adults. I would have to get to a table and ask someone for help. With only partial feelings in my hands, it was likely I would pour juice on the table.

A couple appeared at the side of me and I realised they had come down the flight of stairs from what must be the bar area. They were carrying their pints of lager/beer. This was obviously what adults did. I looked at the stairs to see if I could climb them. There was no hand-rail. There was the top of the wall a little over a metre high, on the right hand side. It was not something that could easily be grasped. You certainly could not get your hand around it. Beyond that there was a door, which had to be opened towards you at the top of the stairs. I knew with a sinking feeling that my body could not manage the stairs. I needed a hand-rail, at least one. In addition, I would have to balance on my legs at the top of the flight and open a door handle. Even if I had been able to be successful in achieving that, I would have to balance well enough to walk to the bar, dealing with any other steps, corners, obstacles on the way. Once there, stand and wait until I could order a drink. The next obstacles were opening the zip on my bag, then my purse and grasp hold of the coins to pay for my drink. Somehow, I would have to then carry the glass full of liquid back down to the play-room. I knew that my body was simply not capable. I felt defeated and alone in a room full of people. Would anyone ask me if I needed help of any kind? I did not feel able to balance on my legs or interrupt any of the groups of chatting people to ask for help. No one came to offer me help, so I just stayed thirsty and longed for the whole thing to be over. I was in such pain and sought to distract myself as best I could.

Peter returned after some time, this time we both needed the toilet. I now knew there was no way I could get upstairs to the adult toilets so I would have to use the tiny children's ones. This time when I opened the door to the toilets, I discovered that there was a leak somewhere, as the floor had become wet and the water was a few centimetres deep. We paddled our way into one of the toilet cubicles. I had the same problem as before with the door lock but this time I knew I would succeed. I managed not to fall with the stupidly low toilet and we both successfully left the room. People began leaving, as Peter went to play one last time. I longed for my husband to arrive with Luke. He did not. All the parents and children left one by one. This included the host who apologised, explaining she had to leave due to another commitment. I was so relieved when my husband finally arrived. Yet this was not the end! I had to balance once more to step back across the threshold to get outside. Peter and Luke were happy to be reunited and ran ahead in great joy with my husband in quick pursuit. I was left on my own, to try and balance on my legs and make them walk up the slope to the car. It was really difficult and painful. I was utterly exhausted when I finally made it. Someone I don't remember who, commented on my being very slow and I was so angry! I was cross I was struggling, cross I was in pain, cross with the footpath and design of the premises throughout! I just wanted to escape, but I could not! Amazingly, I managed not to explode in the car in front of the children, but in my head I went on and on, about how "stupid" everything was.

In hind-sight, I believe the hospital sent me home too soon, before my hands and feet could cope successfully with daily life. Yet I had been so delighted to go home. I simply trusted their judgement and gladly went home.

That night my husband took Luke across to his parent's home, for him to stay the night. This meant that when my husband left in the early hours for his

Sunday job, I would not have to rush looking after my lovely little son. Peter stayed at home with me. I have recorded that we went to church, but failed to say who gave us a lift. I wonder if it were Pam, as I remember she did help in giving me lifts this way, even though she did not live nearby. I also wonder if this were the Sunday when my Church family gave me their condolences. Obviously I do not know what had been said whilst I was away in hospital, but it became apparent that everyone knew by now about the diagnosis of MS and my recent second stay in hospital.

After this certain Sunday morning service, I was sat near the back of church, when people started to come to me and formed a sort of queue. Each person said how they were sorry to hear about my illness and offered to help me if I needed help. I felt like I must be about to die. I had no idea what to say to people. I did not know their names, yet they all knew mine. Nor did I know what kind of help I might need? There was an overwhelming feeling of grief and sorrow and that was from everyone, as well as me. I wanted to escape, but where to? This was my body and it was frightening me. People were expressing their love for me, but at the time it just felt threatening. There was just one woman who made the difference. I did not know her personally, she was a face in the congregation to me. This lady came to me and gave me the weekly notice sheet on which she had written her first name and telephone number. She asked me to contact her and ask her to do anything for me. She wanted to give me any practical support she could. She spoke with a calm authority that somehow was not threatening. I did not know her, and yet felt as though I somehow did.

I had developed a lot of spots on my face that day. I did not know that was a side effect of the steroids at that time. It was yet another symptom I had to learn to live with!

Later that afternoon Jack, a former work colleague and long term friend of my husband came. I got to know him too through work and enjoyed his company. He brought his mother-in-law Hilda, who I knew through Church. A previous church I had attended had a deacon who went on to become the Vicar of Hilda's parish in Leeds. I had developed an upset stomach before they arrived and was feeling more vulnerable than ever. Yet it was so good to have people so obviously caring for me. I felt so ugly and hated having to stand and leave the room with all my stupid struggling to stand and move on full display. I did not know what to do with myself. Yet similar to my Father, between them they brought a bit of calming peace. Hilda was especially calm and matter of fact, as though she had seen it all before, though she said not. I wonder now what she had seen, in order to remain the calming presence she was. Perhaps it was experiences from the war. As she has now gone to be with the Lord, I will just have to wait to find out.

My husband took a week's domestic leave to help in this first week out of hospital. I still had such conflicting emotions and did not want him to be at home because I now had MS. On the other hand I needed his help, with the boys more than anything. I simply could not physically run after them and they were lovely bundles of fun, as they are at that age. Peter could understand that I was ill and manage not to run or bang into me for a short while before he forgot. Luke understood when I told him, but then he would completely forget seconds later and carry on as normal. I did not want to fall over them or hurt them in any way and this used to worry me at that time.

On Tuesday 30th September I had a visit from two Occupational Therapists at home. They had been passed my details from Pinderfield's hospital and had come to see how I was managing at home. I was referred for a wheelchair assessment. I was horrified!

I was still thirty three years old! I did not want a wheelchair! Yet they and my husband thought it a good idea to have in case of need. He said how it would be good to go around a shopping centre or park as I could no longer walk any longer distances. I had not been able to walk to Peter's school or the Doctor's surgery for weeks now. I wanted to walk so much, and once more felt cheated out of my family life. I felt I had to go for the assessment whenever it arose, as all of the arguments presented to me made sense. I muttered lots of "stupids" in my head. The MS was stupid, the stairs were stupid and virtually everything I could think of was stupid!

I have recorded that I reduced down to 20mg of Prednisolone as per my Consultant's instructions. I also saw my GP that day concerning the spots. It was then I discovered that they were a result of the steroids, and I simply had to wait for them to heal on their own. I asked for another sick note to send into work. Ever since I had been unable to work, I had been given a note to cover me for a two week period. This time I was shocked when I read the form as the GP had put six weeks! I cried on the inside, as this clearly meant from a medical point of view, they were not expecting a fast recovery. My husband had taken me to the Doctor's Practice by car, and when I was upset on the journey home, he pointed out the benefit of not having to visit the GP so often. I felt so hurt, I did not want to be disabled and living in pain anymore! I did not feel able to truly cry, as I did not feel he really understood, and yet I knew he was trying.

On Wednesday 1st October my husband dropped me off at a hairdressers in town. I described what I wanted to the hairdresser, but I did not get it. I wished I had managed to get hold of a picture I liked from a magazine, but I had not. I don't remember it exactly now, just that it was another "stupid" to say in my head. I have recorded that the pins and needles were flushing down my spine that day. That was and has remained unpleasant, whenever it has occurred. I felt ravaged by the pins and needles, which seemed worse.

It was around this time when a friend of my sister Becky, passed a message on for me. She was a strong Christian woman called Angela. Whenever I had met her, she was always full of the joy of the Lord and constantly thanked the Lord verbally. She constantly praised Him for every small good thing that happened. Angela had prayed and the message I received from Becky was that Angela believed God was going to heal me. So that was it, God knew there was no way I could doubt three unrelated different sources of his promise to heal me. Perhaps I could doubt one but not three. So once again I had confirmation that God would heal me - but when?

By Thursday 2nd October, my breathing was laboured once more as I was squeezed around my ribs. I have recorded that I saw my Consultant that day. I was still on the reducing dose of Prednisolone, now 20mg per day. I have not recorded that any action was taken. It was the House Group that night. It was by now always held at my home, which made it easier for me. I enjoyed this time with my friends, who all encouraged me and prayed for me. I did my best to listen to what was going on in their lives too and support them, but as I was so consumed by the MS it was difficult focusing on anything else, yet I tried.

It may have been that day when I finally called the lady from Church. I had thought it to death. I thought through all the arguments for calling and asking for help, and all those against. My thoughts were full of wanting independence, and yet I realised I needed help. I don't even remember the exact nature of the need, although it may have been help with collecting the boys from school. Whatever it was, I kept remembering her words to me and so eventually I rang. Sarah was delighted I rang. She had been distracted that morning for no apparent reason and now felt that I was the reason. I discovered she lived in Pontefract, so was not living close by, but she made it clear she had a strong desire to help.

I did not know at the time, but God had put me on her heart. I needed to truly know of His great love for me. Sarah set out to see that that was exactly what I got from her. She was an ordinary busy mum with grown up children of her own at home, the youngest of whom was a teenager at school. She had her own difficulties, and yet she took me on and loved me for the Lord.

Sarah invited me to go to Pontefract Evangelical Church with her on Friday mornings. They had a coffee morning with a guest ten minute preacher, who spoke whilst you drank free coffee or tea and enjoyed a biscuit or two. I was not sure I liked the sound of it, but Sarah gently persuaded me to give it a try. I could not go immediately as my sister Christine was coming to visit so we arranged to go the following week. I am happy to say that whatever physical or mental need I had in the next few years, Sarah set out to meet it with the love of Christ.

October 3ʳᵈ came and my sister Christine called to visit. We went to Ikea and had lunch there. I still hated going around the shop in a wheelchair, and yet I could now see I was able participate more. It was good to get out and I think my sister realised this, long before I did.

By Saturday 4ᵗʰ October I was taking just 10mg of Prednisolone per day. The day brought another children's party for Peter at the same soft play area as last time! I was mentally prepared this time for the difficulties that lay ahead. Once more my husband took Luke with him to do the weekly shop. Once more I endured the tremendous amount of physical pain I was in, with a mass of pins and needles flushing around my body. The children cried out screams of delight as they played. Inside I was struggling to handle the pain and torment it was causing me. At least I was not quite as numb as last week, so there was no getting stuck in the toilets as my hands worked a little better this time around. Everything was still too low and it remained very difficult to cope with. How do disabled people manage? I wondered, do they come to places like this?

The next day brought another children's party, this time at 'Cheeky Chimps' at a shopping centre called

'Freeport'. This was thankfully all level access from the car, and it was level access inside too, apart from two steps. The play area was in the centre and the seats for those watching went around three sides. This meant that parents were not so squashed together and I did not feel quite as exposed. Peter by now knew he loved soft play areas, and children's parties and he rushed off to play. My husband decided to go shopping and thankfully took Luke with him. I was angry inside. I wanted to go shopping, but I could not manage to walk around! I found myself jealous of my husband. I did not know what to do with myself, the pain was so strong and the pins and needles had remained at the same intensity for days now. I am not sure what I had with me in my bag to entertain myself, but I learned that I enjoyed watching Peter playing happily.

Eventually Peter came needing the toilet. It was only those two steps to climb but there was nothing to hold onto, so consequently I struggled, which made me cross again. Peter did not wait for me to return to my seat afterwards. He just rushed off into the play area and I felt stranded and exposed on all this wide open wooden flooring. I suddenly felt scared, it looked so intimidating, all this space and nothing to hold onto. The wooden floor looked as though it would hurt were I to fall on it. I walked as best I could back to the table where I had sat and managed it without falling.

Eventually of course, I wanted a drink. I noticed there was a hot drinks machine towards the toilets up the two steps. Why did it have to be up the two steps? I thought to myself. I decided to be brave and balance on those things called my legs again, over to the vending machine. I made it, even though some children rushing past me, almost caused me to fall. I felt a great sense of achievement when I got there.

Next there was the task of obtaining the drink from the machine. Whilst stood, I was using the stick to help me balance as I read the choices. Once I made my choice I had to balance without using the stick whilst I reached into my bag for my purse. That was really hard and I kept grabbing the machine, every time I nearly lost my balance. Once I had my purse, there was the difficulty of unzipping it. My fingers still found it hard to grasp and pull the zip. Taking longer than I would have liked, I finally managed it. Then I had the problem of grabbing a coin and lifting it out of my purse and putting it in the machine. It was so hard! Anyone who wishes to see what this is like, can do so by putting on a pair of gloves, then trying to grasp coins! Finally I managed it and pressed the appropriate button and my hot chocolate was coming out of the machine into a cup. Great I thought, until I found I could not lift the cup out of the pincer hands that held it in place! When fit and well, I had trouble on the odd occasion when using such a machine. It was nigh impossible now! Yet there was my drink and I was thirsty and so determined to get it. I kept trying to lift it out and spilling some more in the process, but I refused to give up. Finally my grasp held strong enough for me to get it from the machine and to my mouth to drink. What an achievement! Now the last hurdle was getting back to the table, down those two steps, with the added difficulty of a hot drink in my hand.

I had begun to shake involuntarily by this time. I did not realise at that stage of the MS, but the longer I stood, the more tired, my muscles became, and so they would begin to cause me to shake. Carrying the hot drink suddenly seemed impossible. I realised I could not do it! I gave out an internal cry of "help!" to God who heard, even though I did not instantly realise it. Just then there was a man at my side. No it was not my husband, but I was so thankful. He took the drink from my hand without asking first, having seen me struggle. He said something along the lines of he hoped I didn't mind and walked back with me to my table and set the drink down and left. It was such a relief!

I am so thankful to whoever it was, even to this day. Not only did he preserve my dignity, he did not ask if I would like help, he just took the initiative and took the cup from my hand. I am glad he did not ask first, as the words "No thank you", always came to my lips, even when I needed help at the hospital. He seemed to understand what was needed at that point, better than my husband, who was shopping! I really enjoyed the hot chocolate, and I avoided falling over. As I look back now, I believe God was truly looking after me in that situation. I could not have managed to get back to my table without spilling a lot, if not all of the drink. It was highly likely that I would have fallen trying to do so. I did not know what to do, as I stood there shaking by the machine. I see today that God heard my cry and immediately sent an answer.

In due time my husband arrived back with Luke and I went back to feeling cross as he had bought something! He explained this had been difficult with two year old Luke, but it just did not seem fair to me. I was glad he had to do some work, carrying Luke around as we had somehow managed to forget the pushchair. Yet now I wanted the pushchair to lean on for myself, as my muscles were so shaky and I could barely walk. Yet again I was left unattended, as the children raced off, with my husband in hot pursuit. Once more, I muttered under my breath lots of "stupid". Stupid soft play area being too far from the car park, stupid car park with too many cars in, oh there were endless 'stupid' reasons I could think of. It makes me laugh as I look back now. At that time, I wondered if I would ever laugh again? I am so happy the Lord has really blessed me with the gift of laughter over the years, especially being able to laugh at myself. I have learned the truth that "The joy of the Lord is your strength." (Nehemiah 8:10)

After this party we drove across to my in-laws to go out for lunch together. 'On public display in pain again, looking ridiculous', I thought to myself. I am so thankful now when I look back, as it meant that I did not have to cook, or entertain the boys when I was so utterly exhausted! We went to a family pub near Huddersfield. The pins and needles remained the same ferocious strength and still troubled me. I do not remember what any of us ate. The overriding memory is of feeling so ill and yet somehow coping.

Monday 6th October saw me start to receive another source of help. I was not physically able to take Peter to school and Luke to nursery. I had received help from other mums but was desperate to do this job myself. I really wanted to take Peter to school, to spend that precious time with him immediately before school. It felt so important to me at that time. I needed to achieve it, but how? I remember talking with the Vicar about it. He surprised me by offering to help me, until I found another solution. Starting that Monday, the Vicar came to my house every weekday morning, at 8.30am. He would take, Peter, Luke and I to the infant school. He would walk around to Peter's classroom with me and wait for Luke and I. Then he would take us back home. It really made a huge difference to me. I was frustrated that I needed help and yet, so happy to be able to take Peter to school myself. This feeling overrode all others. I remain thankful to this day, for the help provided. I do not think I could have coped without this need being met. At the end of the day I was mum. I desperately wanted to do my job as mum and the Vicar enabled me to do this. Whilst it felt as though my life had fallen apart, he enabled me to hold on to this one vital role. Peter was brought home each day by other mums at this same period of time, this invaluable help kept me going, whilst a more permanent solution was sought.

Later that day my parents came and my Dad took me to Pontefract hospital for my first Physiotherapy appointment since being discharged. I thought it was really 'stupid' at the time. I was in so much pain and I knew that Physiotherapy would hurt. I did not want to increase the amount of pain I already had. How could you possibly do exercises when you could hardly walk? It seemed ludicrous and yet I knew there was a chance it could help, so of course I went. The Physiotherapist assessed me and gave me a series of exercises to do, and some exercises to do at home, until I next saw him. The exercises all felt unnatural, and yet I knew that my legs and body were supposed to move in the way he demonstrated. I felt like some kind of alien, trying to force my body to move in the way it was supposed to, a way it did not want to go. What had my body become?

The days rolled on with the pins and needles still remaining at an angry level. Tuesday 7th October came and the Vicar called and collected the boys and myself again. Our new routine, quickly became established. My sister Becky visited that day with my youngest nephew at that time. Her visit brought welcome relief from my thought life and I enjoyed spending time with her as ever.

On Wednesday 8th October, my walking was a little better. I recorded this again on Friday 10th. What a slight reprieve! Was this the beginning of the end of the MS? I was by now on just 5mg of Prednisolone per day and I wondered if this would affect my body negatively or not? I did not know the answer and I realised by now that actually no one else knew the answer either.

That Friday Sarah took me to Pontefract Evangelical Church again. We went to the market or other shops first and the Christian book shop too again. I had not known that Pontefract had a Christian bookshop, so that had been a pleasant surprise and I enjoyed going every time. The shop was small, but packed full with books, music and gifts. It was a wonderfully calm and peaceful environment and I really enjoyed looking around there every time we went. I frequently wondered if my legs would hold me up, but with Sarah's physical support when necessary, and the odd chair supplied by staff I managed, and I rested during the talk in the Church whilst enjoying the free coffee and biscuits. The ten minute talk was essentially the gospel message. This was presented in many ways, by the different speakers, who appealed to every kind of man's nature. I found some of my belief's were challenged. I was not aware of any wrong thinking I had at that time. I was uncomfortable with this at first as it seemed somehow threatening. Yet on the other hand it seemed safe to continue attending and I really enjoyed spending time with Sarah. She was a steady rock, no matter what problem arose as a result of the MS.

Afterwards, we walked to a café for a jacket potato lunch. Here Sarah and I would talk and she would encourage me in my faith walk. I felt so lost and alone, and Sarah worked hard to give me some security and show me the love of the Lord in every way possible. She really bent over backwards to help me and really was a 'God send'.

I bought myself a new Bible at some point in the first year of MS. It was the New Living Testament Promise Bible. In it, all of God's promises are highlighted throughout the Bible in blue type, so they stood out on the page. When I looked back at my records to write this book, I was happy to see I had bought a notebook in that first year of MS. Encouraged by Sarah, I copied lots of God's promises from the Bible into this book. I did not realise it at the time, but I was beginning to feed my faith.

On Saturday11th October I have recorded my husband and I went to the White Rose Shopping Centre to buy wedding outfits for the boys. It is likely the boys were with their grandparents. I was excessively tired and now know in hind-sight, that I attempted to do too much. I was desperate to choose the outfits with my husband for them to wear at a family wedding. As it turned out, we saw parts of what we liked, but the store did not have the correct sizes so we could not purchase the outfits. I was disappointed as I pushed myself to walk and thought I might faint and we came away without the whole matching outfits. I felt cheated, so much had been taken away from me. I was desperate to be involved in choosing the outfits. I was so disappointed I had not managed to achieve this when the struggle to walk had been so intense. I really fought my body, to last through the rest of the day until it was time for bed when I could escape the physical and mental pain.

I found that I longed for bed every day. My body was at its best first thing in the morning after a good night's sleep. As the day progressed I became more tired and painful. The symptoms would deteriorate further, which was always frightening as I did not know at what stage the symptoms would stop. My legs threatened daily that they would fail to hold me up.

This threat increased as each day wore on. I was afraid that my legs would give way whilst I was out of the house. What would I do if that happened? I was afraid they would give way in the house as I sought to do all the necessary jobs as housewife and mother. I learned gradually to recognise the signals that my legs were about to give out and that I simply had to stop doing the jobs before that time and sit down or sleep. It took a long time before I got this right. I consequently had to spend time sat on the floor in the hall or in another location, until my legs recovered sufficiently to get to the couch or the bed depending on where I was in the house.

I do not remember exactly when, but during the summer, it was necessary for me to sleep every afternoon for an hour. This seemed to help me regain some energy. After the sleep I could continue. I would typically lie down just before 2pm. Even with this hours sleep before tea each day, I would wonder if I could last until bed time? I learned that each evening meal would give me a boost, which helped me to get through the evening until I collapsed into bed. Life was one enormous struggle to get through, both physically and mentally.

At that time, my Church held Sunday evening services. Sometimes, these were Communion Services, sometime Praise Services. Sarah took me to these to help boost my faith. Sometimes my legs refused to stand and so Sarah would put my arm around her neck and her arm around my waist to help to hold me up. I really wanted to stand, at every point in the service where you are supposed to, and Sarah made that possible. I made friends with Sarah's teenage daughter Louise and when she came, at times they both held me up. When I look back now, I see just how blessed I was. I was praying for God to help me. I wanted immediate healing. I did not see that he was giving me all the support I needed to live through this chapter of my life with Sarah and sometimes Louise too. I did not keep a detailed diary at that time but each occasion that cropped up, God has reminded me of details. Sarah was there for me at the end of the phone. She was there for me physically every Friday and Sunday and sometimes in between. There are no words to truly express how much she blessed me. I was and am extremely thankful for her help and love. I pray everyone, who needs one, gets a 'Sarah'.

It was now Monday 13th October. Another week began and the interminable struggle continued. I have written in my diary that Peter had a school disco straight after school. How could I attend when I was in such pain, and walking was so difficult? If I did make it, what could I do with Luke? I decided to go struggling, and managed to attend with Luke for Peter, who really wanted to go to his first disco. At the end of the day I am a mum, and I wanted the children to be happy, so I frequently struggled to achieve things for them both.

The following day it was time for the school photograph to be taken. My husband took the boys to this. The school took their photograph together too, even though Luke was not a pupil. Every time my husband took a day off, or went into work late, it made such a positive difference for me. It does not sound like a huge event as I type this, but every act like this helped me to manage and continue living in what seemed like impossible circumstances.

9 - Celebrating with MS

Wednesday 15th October 2003 was my 34th birthday. Birthday's are usually joyous celebrations and here I was feeling so far from joy, consumed by physical and mental pain. I didn't want it to be my birthday, I felt cheated! I had lost my life, how could I celebrate my birthday? I have written in my diary that my parents took me out for a Mexican lunch which I will have enjoyed as I like spicy food. I do not remember the actual occasion. I learned some time after that occasion, that my Father dislikes any kind of spicy food, so he really went out on a limb for me. My parents did everything they could to help me and encourage me in every way, providing just what I needed.

The next event was a wedding in my husband's family in Edinburgh. Once more I felt trapped. I still felt really ill and not well enough to travel up to Edinburgh and certainly not well enough to function at a wedding and make it to the end of the day. Yet I wanted to be with the boys who looked gorgeous in their matching outfits. I wanted to be a part of my larger family, and so I set my mind to go.

It was Friday 17th October and we collected my husband's parents and all travelled together with my husband driving our car. We broke the journey in Newcastle at Sheila and Sam's home. Sheila blessed us with a lunch with her and Sam for all six of us. I had voiced my many concerns to her about travelling when I was so ill. Sheila wanted to help me and she really did. The only down side was that it made the day last so much longer, which I found hard. I was so glad when we reached the hotel. I have no recollection of what the accommodation was like, or what we ate. My thoughts were simply fixed on making it through the experience.

The following day was the wedding itself. I really tried hard to be happy in the midst of the pain and do more than simply live through the day. This is the first time I remember earnestly trying to find pleasure amidst the pain. I looked at the boys and aged 2 and 5, they looked adorable, which was a big help. I found if I could try and keep focused on them, I did have some success. I began to share the delight of the boys with my mother-in-law, which she also enjoyed. I kept giving myself 'pep talks', to encourage myself. I had become increasingly time obsessed, as I sought to make it through each hour of the day. I asked God to help me and He enabled me to see the joy of the boys through the veil of pain. They were the best possible distraction. I also grew closer to my mother-in-law through the boys and sharing the joy of them with her. The day was a very long one for me, but I could see there were brief moments of joy amidst the torture. The Bride and Groom had a wonderful experience as they should and the day finally came to an end.

On the Sunday we visited a famous Italian Delicatessen in Edinburgh. By this time, I just wanted to go home. Yet I knew despite my anxiety about reaching home, that our final arrival would not mean an end to the pain. Yet a return to familiar surroundings, is what I desired. I simply had to wait. I longed for my husband to understand. I wanted him to see the degree of difficulty I had and the immense pain I was in. Yet he did not see, and he did not understand. It was a long journey home, yet I survived.

Monday 20th October arrived and it was the school half-term holidays. I have recorded that we went to my sister Becky's house, visiting a children's soft play area first. I believe she collected us in her car. The boys were only too happy to be able to play with their cousins. It was good for the boys to enjoy a good time playing as there was so little I was capable of doing with them. At every school holiday I wondered what on earth I could do to keep them entertained? Being in this state of constant illness was very limiting. I could not walk as far as the park. I rarely tried to walk to the nearer small playground on the estate now, as that was too far as well. I wondered time and time again how I was supposed to manage my two and five year old boys in this poor physical condition. I believe now that God gave me the strength and support I needed to do just that.

On Tuesday 21st October the Council came and fitted the external hand rails at the front of the house. "That was it", I thought, "I was advertising I was disabled and no longer able to function normally!" I felt like I might as well just shout it out from the roof tops. I still wasn't ready. I have no idea what I said to the workman? I was in shock. It seemed so recent still, and yet I remember him as a caring chap. He fitted two rails by the front door and one by the back door too. He also fitted one in the shower. It helped somehow that he showed compassion to me, even though he did not know me from Adam.

Luke became ill on that day with a vomiting bug. How could I clean up after him and take care of him properly, when I was exhausted and struggled to move across the room with the MS? Now what would I do? Thankfully my parents arrived. They were able to clean up after Luke, and do all things that were necessary so much easier than I. Once more, although I could not see it at the time, the Lord was providing me with the support I needed. The following day my husband took the day off so he could look after Luke. I am grateful that he had a job, with some degree of flexibility. Where his employers were understanding about my condition, and allowed him to take annual leave on such occasions, when problems like children's illnesses cropped up. Being a Leeds lass, I am proud to say that Leeds City Council were good to us, at the time when we needed it the most.

On Thursday 23rd Peter had a Speech Therapy assessment at the health centre. How would I get there I wondered? Thankfully, the bus to Wakefield came close by, just a five minute walk from our house at that time. I could manage that distance then. It stopped further on it's windy route, right outside the Health Centre. I was able to make it to the Health Centre with Peter and at the right time too. The bus times amazingly fitted in for the journey home too.

Given that there was just one bus an hour, this was really good! I did my best not to worry about Peter's stammer, which started shortly after he began school. I could not help but wonder if it was somehow related to the stresses the MS had put upon our family?

Later that morning my Father collected us and we went across to their home in Leeds for lunch and the afternoon. It did me good to get away from the house. The boys enjoyed themselves exploring and playing there and there were no jobs for me to do there. My parents provided invaluable help to me as ever.

On Friday 24th October I finally finished the reducing dose of steroids. What did that mean? What would happen next? I was already feeling stressed that day as Personnel were visiting me at home. What could I say to them? I still had no idea when I would be well enough to go back to work? I still could not function properly at home and there was no doubt that I was not physically capable of carrying out my job.

I believe that it went as well as it could have. The outcome was that I was given longer to recover and would be reassessed at a later date. I was extremely concerned about my job by this time. When would I recover? I found not knowing very difficult to handle.

I made it to the next day again. My sister Christine was up visiting the family that weekend which I enjoyed. We did the usual visit to my in-laws. There Luke happily stayed overnight. This really helped me as my husband left in the early hours to work at his Sunday job. Peter was much easier to take care of as he could be left unattended at times whilst I got up, or completed a task of some kind. On Sunday afternoon my husband went and collected Luke whilst I had my much needed afternoon nap. My in-laws were a real blessing every time they had either one, or even both boys. They thoroughly enjoyed it too.

I saw a GP the next day. I had developed an itchy rash. At that time the only medication I was taking was Oxybutinin. I had been started on this whilst in hospital as it was noted how I went too frequently to empty my bladder. I could not tell if I were going any more frequently than before? I was informed by more than one staff member that MS often causes an overactive bladder so I took the medicine. Now the GP changed me onto an alternative, Propiverine.

It felt as the world continued to race around and I just wanted everything to stop, at least for a little while. This did not happen and on Wednesday 29th October I attended the Crohn's clinic at Leeds General

Infirmary. I wondered if they might be able to help me in some way? It is most likely that my father took me, as my mobility was still very poor. Of course this team of Doctor's showed great empathy, but they were unable to offer me any more help.

Later that same day my mother was admitted to St James' Hospital in Leeds, with a stomach bleed and suspected stomach ulcer. I could not rush to her side. I had no way of getting to the hospital on my own, I needed my husband to take me! This became a frustrating common problem where I was limited by the MS. I wanted to be there for my mother. Yet the MS would not allow that. As a mother myself, I also needed to be there for the school runs and fix my attention on making it through each day. I was emotionally torn and there seemed nothing I could do about it.

On Saturday 1st November a neighbour a few houses down the street invited me for coffee. This was a real blessing and I enjoyed my time with her. She was a compassionate woman who listened and offered help should I need it. Other people's kindness always made me feel better emotionally. It was as a small sugar in the bitter drink of my life. Yet again the Lord provided refreshment as I needed it, even though I could not clearly see His hand at work at that time. My mother had recovered well enough from her stomach bleed to be discharged later that day. That same day I also managed to walk around the supermarket for the first time in months. I struggled but it felt so good to achieve it. I subsequently found it extra difficult to get through the following day as a result of pushing myself, but at least it was the weekend so my husband was there to help.

The weekend was soon over and the school routine began again. The Vicar collected the boys and I enabling me to take Peter to school once more. Another mum collected Luke and I and took us to playgroup. She brought me home whilst he was at playgroup so I was able to get on with the washing, or whatever other chores there were to do. Then she would return to collect me and our children from playgroup at the end of the session. I had all the help I needed and yet I was still fearful of the MS, what would happen next and how I would manage?

On Tuesday 4th November the toes in my right foot had gone numb. I tried not to panic as I realised I could not stop what was happening, yet the fear was intense. My husband took me to Physiotherapy as my father was ill.

Bonfire Night arrived the next day and I usually really enjoyed this celebration. I have always enjoyed firework displays and since we had the boys, I enjoyed seeing them happy too. Now however, just like my birthday, it seemed all wrong. The joy had been sucked out of the occasion and pain seemed to take its place. I still wanted to celebrate and Peter really wanted to celebrate too.

I invited two of our friendly neighbours around to join in the occasion. We bought a box of family fireworks, suitable for small children. In spite of the pain, I was able to enjoy myself a little. I was so glad the neighbours came, although I did not think to provide food. It did not occur to me to buy food as I was simply focused on making it through each day. I think they understood when I apologised, once I realised my lack of forethought. My youngest son was not so excited about the event and managed to sleep through it all!

My husband took me to see my Consultant the next day before he went to work. The numbness was increasing. To my dismay the Consultant said it was too early to say if it were a relapse or not and did nothing! I somehow imagined that there would be some kind of action taken at the beginning of a relapse to stop the condition developing further. I was so disappointed to see that it was not the case.

The numbness continued to get steadily worse each day. I was consumed by fear. Would it get as bad as the last two times? Would I still be able to walk? What would happen if I could not use my hands? In one sense that had been worse because you need to eat and drink and be able to use your hands for many every day functions. It had been one tremendous struggle last time and I did not want to have to endure that again. 'What did other people in this situation do?' I wondered.

The days rolled on and the MS continued to torment me without reprieve. My husband received an unexpected call on Sunday 9th asking him to work that day at his Sunday job. He decided to go, so I was left to manage the two boys on my own. This felt threatening and yet I had managed so many times before. It was Remembrance Sunday, so there was no appropriate service at Church to take the boys to. We stayed at home. They liked painting and playdough, at that age so I may have entertained them with that, part of the day. As pain increased with walking, I tried to limit the walking if possible. This was not often achieved, especially if they made a mess or wanted to play something like hide and seek. In the afternoon, I needed to sleep for an hour and thankfully they were responsible enough to watch a DVD. They would choose one which I would start to play. I would then go and lie down and they would wake me up when the DVD finished. I was always still tired on waking, however I was not cross as they were two happy boys invariably jiggling about at the side of the bed, excited at whatever event was coming next. Each day ran into the next, without my having any control over my symptoms, so I was consequently filled with an ever present fear.

On Tuesday 11th November, I saw a GP as my sick note ran out. This Doctor gave me a note for two months. I was upset as last time. I did not want to be ill for one minute longer! I wanted my life back! I could not have it and still did not know when I would get back to work? I began to wonder if the Doctor's thought I would make it back to work? The length of the sick note was longer, did that mean they thought I was stuck in this time period in this condition? It was too frightening to think that way, so I did my best not to and just focused on making it through each day. I felt very low at this point and I moaned a lot in my head about it. "How low do I have become, before things get better? How ill do I have to be? How much suffering must I endure?" Then it dawned on me that I was talking to myself and not sharing what was in my head with God. Sarah had been encouraging me to share everything with the Lord, and I am sure she will not have been the only one. When I prayed I felt such relief as the burden was shared. I wondered then, if God were fed up with me moaning? So I picked up my Bible and opened it. It opened in the book of Psalms on number 69 and my eyes fell on verse 33, "For the Lord hears the cries of his needy ones; He does not despise his people who are oppressed." Wow! It seemed so unlikely, and yet it happened! That meant God was not mad at me or disappointed with me either? That seemed so strange as I had believed those negatives for a long time. The truth seemed a little scary so I chose not to dwell on it.

On Thursday 13th November Peter had a Speech Therapy class. My Father came across and took us. I hoped Peter would recover from the stammer. I learned the starting of school for a child, is a common time for a stammer to appear. There is no quick fix solution. Instead Peter had to learn to recognise his own speech patterns and learn coping mechanisms and strategies to alleviate the stammer. It made no difference if I thought the MS and my ill health was a trigger which started the stammer. I felt guilty for a while in case that was the truth of the situation. Eventually I learned not to do so, as my feelings changed nothing. A degree of rational common sense crept into my thought life occasionally, and it really helped.

Later that day I had a Doctor visit me at home to assess me to see if I qualified for the benefit, Disability Living Allowance. My employer Leeds City Council, was still paying me. At that time they paid an employee for six months on full pay. The last day I had been able to work had been the 1st August and it was now 13th November. I was concerned at the amount of time that had passed by without my being able to return to work.

This Doctor explained that he was no longer practising as a Doctor, but worked carrying out health assessments like mine. I asked lots of questions and I remember having to lead him around the house and demonstrate my climbing the stairs. He was thorough in his questioning and at the end asked me if I had any questions? I surprised him when I asked about the constant pins and needles and if that might ever stop? He reiterated that he was no longer practising medicine as such, but I wanted his opinion none-the-less. My Consultant had told me that I would have to live with the pins and needles as they were. He did not expect to see any improvement. That seemed very harsh to me, as they were so strong. I hoped that they may reduce and even go altogether, when my condition improved. This Doctor could see my concern and answered with compassion. In his experience he believed that the strength and duration could fluctuate. He gave me a dose of hope with his answer and it was gratefully received. I hoped I would qualify for DLA, but like everything else, it seemed very much a wait and see affair.

The next day I was a little better and wondered if that meant the deterioration was slowing down? I was frustrated by my lack of understanding of this disease and my own symptoms. Of course I could see some patterns emerging by now and I was learning what actions to avoid, or try to reduce which exacerbated the symptoms.

My body wanted me to rest, but there was too much to do. The more washing, cleaning and other jobs I did, the worse the exhaustion became. That meant it was harder to drag my body around for the rest of the day. I would stumble more and become even less coordinated in my movements. I had for some months been smashing plates and bowls and glasses. This was a never ending regularity as my grip was no longer solid. It was like holding items whilst wearing a pair of gloves again. I found that generally speaking, I could still hold things but I could not tell how hard I was grasping, and was unable to grasp things really firmly, the power was not there anymore. Smashing things meant more work, pain and risk, having to bend over to pick up and vacuum up. That fuelled my internal anger. I was angry with myself and angry with the life I had lost. At least I still maintained the ability to use my hands. Yet I did not know if or when they would get as numb as in the second relapse? Countless "What if's" crowded my mind. Fear tightened its grip.

I was relieved that Saturday night when Peter stayed with my in-laws again. Once more I had just one child to deal with in the morning, whilst my husband carried out his Sunday morning job.

On Tuesday 18th November I had my last Physiotherapy session at Pontefract Hospital. The Physiotherapist had instructed me to buy this large exercise ball to continue to carry out certain exercises. I bought the ball and took it with me for him to blow up on the equipment in the Gym. The ball grew and grew and then burst! He was so apologetic. I did not know if it had been his error or if the ball had been faulty. I stated I would buy another, but he would not hear of it and insisted I took an inflated one from the Gym. I did not want to, as either way it had been accidental. Yet he insisted and so I eventually took it. I then had to roll this ball down the hospital corridor and, through double doors, whilst keeping my balance. Of course my Father took charge when he met me and took me home. I had to admit that the Physiotherapy did have a positive effect on my walking and on my balance at that time. I maintained the exercises at home until I was no longer able to do so.

My husband and I agreed that we would raise the children in the Christian faith. Whilst he was not a practising Christian, he believed in the Christian moral principles as a good standard on which to raise the boys. We had agreed that when the boys were old enough to decide for themselves, they could be baptised formally into the Christian faith. Suddenly getting MS, made me not want the boys to wait any longer before being baptised. I desperately wanted to make that decision for them. My husband and I discussed it lots and thankfully he allowed me to make arrangements for this to be carried out. The Baptism visit which all parents are required to have, was arranged for the 1st December. Sadly this had to be cancelled as one of the visitors who would be calling was ill.

Time continued to race by and the MS was deteriorating yet more. I felt so frustrated but there was nothing I could do about it. At least this time the deterioration progressed at a slower pace. Yet I was worried I might have to go into hospital again. I did not want to leave the boys again! Both boys had found it upsetting before and it had taken two months for them to get over the fear of losing me. Luke panicked and became upset every time the word 'hospital' was mentioned. I did not want to be in hospital over Christmas. The House Group specifically prayed for me over this situation.

On Friday 5th December I had an appointment to see a Consultant specialist in 'Beta-Interferon' treatment at Pinderfield's Hospital. I believe Sarah took me. This was one of the countless times she stepped in to provide me with the lift by car and the physical help I needed. The treatment I was informed was by injection that you had to learn to self-administer. I did not like the sound of that, nor having such medicine in the house with two young children. The second problem was that a side effect it gave was flu-like symptoms after the injection. This lasted for just twenty four hours on average. However, in some cases it lasted four or five days. I could not imagine managing to look after my children with flu-like symptoms at all! Certainly, not whilst I was in so much pain with the MS and had such difficulty in moving. I did not feel it would be safe for the boys either. They were a lovely handful who needed supervision and I felt leaving them with a DVD whilst I slept, was already enough of a risk. The Consultant said that the MS attack's could be considered one long attack. He would have to discuss this with his colleagues. He was not sure if the Crohn's Disease was a contraindication to the Beta-Interferon and he stated he would write to me when he had all the information he needed. I discussed all my concerns with the Consultant and I agreed to think more about it and discuss it with my husband. I felt blessed as I was obviously cared for by this Consultant and the NHS as a whole. I was listened to and given choices and this helped me to cope.

Owing to the deterioration in my condition, this Consultant arranged for me to receive Intravenous steroid treatment as a day patient on Ward 2 at Pinderfield's Hospital, starting on Monday. Unfortunately I was ill again. This time I had a bad sore throat and a huge ulcer on my tongue and therefore visited a GP at my local Doctors surgery. I received antibiotics. Sadly my husband was ill with a sore throat too. This illness meant that I could not have the steroid treatment. It was rebooked for the following week. It also meant that the second Baptism visit had to be cancelled, this time by me.

On Tuesday 9th December my parents came to visit and help me in every way they could, even though they put themselves at risk of catching the bug. I felt ill but was so happy to see them. On that day they insisted on taking me to a local shop that sold new and reconditioned mobility scooters. I did not feel well so I did not really want to go. The fact that I did not want a mobility scooter, made it worse. They had an insurance policy that had matured and wanted to buy me a mobility scooter, so that I could go independently to take Peter to school and go to the local shops and park. Eventually I agreed to go, Yet I did not want a mobility scooter! They were for old people and I was thirty-four years old! Yet it made perfect sense, and would give me back some independence. I had to really battle with myself but the thought of being independent once more won in my head in the end. First I tried I tried out a few in the store. Then I tried the best looking and most comfortable one outside the store on the road. I can honestly say I both hated and loved it. It had a black fibre glass frame, with a grey man-made wipe-able seat and its design looked the most modern. I am so thankful my parents bought it for me. I now believe God was chiselling away at my pride and self-reliance.

My new Mobility Scooter meant that the Vicar was relieved of taking myself and the boys to school each weekday morning. The Lord really provided all that I needed. It astonishes me now that I really could not see it at that time! I was effectively blind to it.

I was so relieved to be able to take Peter to school myself with Luke sat on me knee, and yet I hated being on the scooter too. I could not see how I could live with it? I would soon see. There was a retired man who would often be walking back from the shops on an afternoon, as I went to collect Peter from school. This chap when he saw me coming on the mobility scooter, changed his behaviour from the usual cheery 'hello', to something extra special. He began to suddenly jump out ahead in front of me, with his arms outstretched. He had a shopping bag raised in each hand and he blocked the pavement. It was so funny! I laughed out loud! What a relief it was! He did not just bless me with this funny sight once, but did it repeatedly every time he saw me for about a month! That of course, eventually made me look forward to going out on the mobility scooter, in case I would see him and be able to laugh again.

When I look back at this time I see now how God used this man to bless me with the gift of laughter. I really needed it, and it changed my view of the mobility scooter into the blessing it truly was. With a back drop of constant pain I learned how to laugh again. This time in my life still makes me laugh today and I am grateful to the chap concerned. He made such a positive impact on my life, when I truly needed it.

Christmas was getting ever closer and yet I was no closer to being well. I was heading down a pathway of ever increasing numbness. The children's Christmas advent activities began. On 12th December Luke's nursery group received a visit by Santa. I was back to an intense struggle to force my legs to walk. I remember arriving at the venue and not being sure I would make it inside. Thankfully my friend Alice was there, as was her husband. They offered to help me and I immediately grabbed onto Alice's husband's arm. Alice herself was a very slim build, who looked as though she may not be able to hold me up, were I to stumble and fall. I was in survival mode. Her husband helped me to a chair.

The children all sat together on the carpet and 'Santa' called out each name individually. The child went to Santa to collect their gift and then the mother or father collected the child and sat them on their lap. When I realised this, my heart sank. My legs did not want to co-operate at all. I did not want to fall publicly, or accidently hurt anyone else. How could I manage? I prayed asking God to help me stand upright and walk and yet I became increasingly nervous as time passed. When it was Luke's turn I staggered as I got up, but I did not fall. I was able to make it to collect him and then just the hurdle of getting him on my knee remained. Thankfully attention had drifted onto the next child and Luke was able to climb on my knee by himself with little assistance required from my unwieldy body.

I realised the next part of the test was being able to get up and walk, in order to leave the building at the end. I felt as though I was taking an exam and it was essential I passed. When the time came I did not rush but let those in haste leave first. Thankfully Luke was totally unaware of what was going on and once he had his coat on, he just wanted to go home for lunch. I successfully managed to stand. The pain in my legs by this time was tremendous and I remember wondering if I would faint? No one could see the pain and the intense physical struggle, I was alone in it. I asked God to get me safely back to the mobility scooter and He did. For Luke, riding on my knee on the mobility scooter was an exciting adventure. So he eagerly climbed onto my knee with only a guiding largely numb arm to help. I wanted to cry out, the pain was so intense! Yet I could not, as I had to be mum. We made it home and I continued to live out my role.

On Monday 15th I was denied Intravenous steroids again! I had finished the antibiotics but the nurse in charge of the day ward insisted that I could not have steroids and would now have to wait until after Christmas for any treatment. I was desperate as I could barely walk now and knew I needed the treatment now, whilst I could still move. The nurse was adamant and could not see the severity of my condition. She duly booked me in for treatment for the first week in January. I put the telephone down and did not know what to do. I knew at the current rate of deterioration I would not be able to walk a single step by Christmas Day. I did not want to spend Christmas in hospital. What on earth could I do?

On Friday 19th December I was due to see the Consultant specialist in Beta Interferon. I have recorded in my diary that this appointment was cancelled and a new one made for the following March. I have not recorded the reason for the cancellation. It could have been because school finished early that day for the Christmas holidays. I believe I spoke with this Consultant on the telephone and he arranged for me to begin a three day course of Intravenous steroids on Ward 2 beginning on 22nd December. When I later rang Ward 2 I was told to attend at 9.00am. Just a little longer to last until Monday I said to myself.

The very next day my condition deteriorated rapidly throughout the day. I stayed home to rest, but after a two hour sleep in the afternoon, I was barely able to walk even with assistance of my husband. I have recorded it was like trying to balance and walk on stilts once more. This time I was doing a stagger going sideways which I had discovered came more easily than going forwards. I had a lot of pain under each foot as well as though I had a small stone underneath each foot. I needed my husband's help that day and he was as worried as I was. We had a lovely helpful neighbour who came over in the evening to take care of the boys whilst my husband took me to Casualty. I took my hospital bag with me believing I would be admitted.

I waited on my own, once my husband assisted me into a seat in the waiting area. He then went to park the car. A nurse called for me to come through and I had to shout that I needed help, but he did not seem to have heard me. It was another woman in the waiting room sat with her husband/partner who came to my aid. She helped me up and I leaned on her to get into the assessment room. This male nurse lacked good communication skills and made me feel like a number. He failed to listen to what I said, and so I had to repeat myself, as he continued to look at the computer without looking at me. My husband then arrived and joined me. The nurse typed in the necessary information onto the computer and asked us in a monotonous voice, to return to the waiting room until a Doctor called.

I was seen by a Doctor who asked me questions and examined me before he telephoned the on-call Neurologist. The Neurologist informed the Doctor that treatment was not available at weekends, and I should return on Monday. The Doctor passed on this message. My husband was annoyed and politely but firmly expressed the degree of difficulty I had and how it was getting worse each day. The Doctor rang the Neurologist again, this time when he came back, he reported I would have to wait in the assessment unit and it still may not be possible to admit me onto Ward 2. They could give me medicine for pain relief in my feet in the meantime and steroid treatment would begin on Monday if I were admitted or not. I did not know what I should do? The Doctor in Casualty said that I could return the following day, if my symptoms were worse again. From his tone, I think he saw my predicament and wanted to help if he could. The Doctor prescribed Gabapentin for the foot pain and so we returned home. I preferred going home, If I could wait until Monday, I would wait, so that I would not have to be away from the boys. My husband and I both wondered what condition I would be in the following morning. At some point it dawned on me that I should pray, and the Lord answered overnight.

On Sunday 21st December I woke to find there had been a slight change in the condition of my legs overnight. It was still very slow and difficult to move, but there was a slight improvement as if I had travelled back in time a few days. This made me feel I could last until the next day for treatment. I managed to get to Church with Sarah's help. She put my arm around her neck and half carried me as I attempted to stagger up to Church that evening for the Carol service. Another member of the Church family saw us and took my other arm putting it around their neck I was so happy to have made it. I felt fully confident that God was looking after me by this time, and that everything would be alright. I was so happy and had His amazing peace! The Vicar looked so sad when he saw the extent of my struggle. I felt sorry for him. I was happy and found myself giving him a hug when he came near, and telling him I would be alright. I felt I had made it against all the odds!

During the carol service the Crohn's pain suddenly came on strongly. I thought it would spoil things as I sat holding my abdomen. Sarah fetched me some water and prayed advising me to pray, for God to anaesthetise my stomach. That sounded strange to me and I realised I was letting my preconceived ideas get in the way. So I prayed as advised, and after a few minutes the pain was gone! This was not normal for the Crohn's Disease! After the service, people were really kind to me. Several people said they would pray for me to be at home and enjoy Christmas. I made it back to the car again with two helpers half carrying me and I returned happily home. I felt truly safe and cared for and went to bed really happy. I believe I saw God's goodness through many at that time and thanked Him.

When I awoke on Monday morning 22nd December, my legs had returned to the stilt like condition they had been in on Saturday.

My husband took me, half carrying me, with the boys to Ward 2 at 9:00 am. I expected to have 1000mg of Methyl-Prednisolone a day for three days, as before. Unfortunately the staff on Ward 2 declared they knew nothing about it! My husband was annoyed and politely explained my predicament and the episode at Casualty. Panic threatened inside of me and I tried to stay calm as telephone calls were made by one of the nursing staff. I asked my husband to take the boys to my sister's as previously arranged. My husband took the boys and I waited anxiously. At the end of the telephone calls, it had been decided that I would need to see the Doctor on that Ward when he arrived later that morning. I was asked to go to the corner room where I had been as a patient. The Ward clerk helped me to walk to it.

The Doctor duly arrived and tested my muscles for spasticity and watched me walk. He tested my muscle weakness and looked at the degree of numbness I had. I knew I needed treatment and hoped he could see that I needed it too. He advised me that in his opinion I needed the steroid treatment, but that it was dangerous because I would be exceeding the recommended dose which could lead to other health problems like Osteoporosis. I just wanted to walk! I wanted to be able to use my hands to lift a cup safely to my mouth! I wanted to be able to keep going! It was too frightening and too difficult to do so already and I did not want to be admitted. Thankfully, this Doctor arranged for me to receive the first day of treatment on the Ward immediately. In a short space of time I had a cannula put in my hand and was hooked up to the drip and treatment began. My husband then returned to the ward and then left again to go and do some Christmas shopping. I began to come down from the 'red alert' status I had been in.

My Consultant suddenly appeared during this treatment. He publicly shouted at me on the ward, that I was having too many steroid treatments! Then he stormed off. I remember thinking, "What was wrong with that man? How did he expect me walk when my legs refused. How could I cope with two young children if I could not walk or use my hands? It was an easy choice for me, walk or don't walk. How could he possibly consider that too much and why was he always angry with me? I wondered what the other patients thought of his outburst, or Me? What did it matter, I just needed to survive." Once on my own, I remembered to ask the returning Doctor for help as I was not sleeping and asked if he could give me some sleeping tablets. He said he would prescribe me a short course, but it turned out that I had to wait two and a half hours for the prescription!

A problem arose as I was told I could not have the next treatment on Ward 2 the following day. Instead I was asked to attend Ward 3 at 07.30am the next day! As I was so desperate, for the treatment, I said I would fit in with them and agreed before I knew how I would get there.

Thankfully my husband was able to take the boys to my in-laws for the day, before he did more Christmas shopping. On Ward 3 they were too busy at 07.30 and asked me to wait in the patients lounge. I asked if they had forgotten me an hour later, but no I was told, they were simply too busy still. At 11:30 they called me in for treatment. I was placed at the end of the ward in a high backed chair. In the adjoining bed was a teenage girl and her friend. She had a steady stream of Doctors and other people around her when I first arrived. They both stank of cigarettes, as though they had smoked and eaten several packets each in one go. I knew nothing about the girl in the bed but I just knew I was supposed to talk to her. I am shy by nature and

167

struggled to think of something to say, and then to pluck up the courage to get the words to come out of my mouth.

After a few minutes I was successful and said something. The girl readily replied and explained that she had been admitted because she had slashed her wrists. This always made her feel better, when she had become so upset or frustrated by something. She asked about my condition, so I had to explain about the MS. Yet I found myself able to say how being a Christian helped me cope. She was surprised and I was going to say more but something caught her eye on the television and the moment had passed. I wanted to say "Jesus loves you", but I did not get the opportunity. I hoped it would be enough to help her investigate for herself, to find Jesus and not to self-harm again.

It was of course now Christmas Eve. I had the third and final treatment booked for 7:30 am Ward 3. Sarah came to my rescue and got up early to take me. Sarah was great, she was so positive a person and always lifted my spirits. I held onto her and she was a tower of strength to lean into. I was concerned she may not be able to stay on Ward 3, but there was no problem. I wondered if the girl from yesterday would be there but discovered she had been discharged. Today I was put in a chair next to a bed with a middle aged patient who shared that she had terminal cancer. I found myself sharing with her about how much my faith helped and where I stopped, Sarah was able to encourage this woman further. A pensioner in the next bed joined in the conversation and we all chatted in a relaxed manner. After treatment Sarah got me to the canteen and we enjoyed breakfast. I believe she pointed out that God had answered my prayers. I did not have to be away from the boys this time. I was going to wake up and watch them open their presents. Then we were going to have the in-laws with us and the next day go to my mother's where I would enjoy seeing even more of my family. I felt humbled by His goodness. Was He that interested in me? I still felt unsure of His thoughts towards me, but it felt good, when Sarah pointed out He had answered my prayers. I did not understand what was going on, but it gave me a little more hope to hang on to.

10 – The First Christmas with MS

This time the anxiety over celebrating a usually happy event, whilst in so much pain, was a great deal less than on other occasions. That evening when the boys were in bed I found I was not able to wrap as many gifts for them as I wanted to. I tried to do as many as I could, but eventually I had to leave my husband to finish the wrapping on his own. I simply had to sleep I was utterly exhausted once more. I did not like leaving the wrapping. I wanted to be a full part of my family unit. Yet I had no choice in the matter.

On Christmas Day the boys excitement at Christmas was wonderful! Watching them open their many gifts was a real tonic and once more I found that I was able to be happy with them, in spite of the pain. My husband collected his parents who spent most of the day with us. The boys enjoyed the attention lavished upon them. There was little I could do to help apart from making drinks and I was not good at that, given the difficulty in walking. I believe I had the walking trolley by that time, so I was able to put drinks on that which helped me. At least the steroid treatment had stopped the advancement of the symptoms. Life was incredibly hard, but in amongst that, were moments of pure joy.

On Boxing Day we spent the day with my parents as did my sister Becky and all her family. The children had the most wonderful time with their cousins. It was good to spend time with family. My sister Christine travelled up with her family the following day. She spent her time divided amongst different family members as she stayed six days. Joan did not stay with us this time in order not to add to the pain I was in, with noise and extra busyness.

On 29th December I saw a GP who prescribed Gabapentin as in Casualty. I hoped that it would suppress the pain as I found it so hard to bear, although it had made no difference so far. Also that day my youngest son Luke saw another GP. He had been suffering from sudden stomach pains for some weeks. These sudden stomach pains had grown in frequency. This intermittent abdominal pain he suffered, went on for months and eventually he was referred to a Consultant Paediatrician. After numerous tests over more than two years, it was discovered there was no underlying condition. I now believe that Luke was stressed with the MS and the pain was a result of him not being able to communicate his concerns and feelings with us.

Later that day, my sister Becky, threw a surprise 40th birthday party, for my sister Christine. Her birthday had been earlier in the month but it had not been possible to celebrate then. Now all the family came together to celebrate. Becky had invited Christine's friends from school and University. I found it so difficult as the pain was immense and I had to try and socialise. It was hard to function even with family members as well as my sister's friends. I really just wanted to escape. Yet I stayed for Christine's special night for as long as I could. The boys were of course having a wild time with their cousins. After a while I found my Dad and I spent time with him, as he was reassuringly calm. I felt too ill to stay and after approximately two hours, much to the boy's disappointment, at my request my husband brought us all home.

New Year's Eve came and I made no attempt at staying up, I simply felt too ill. The steroids had stopped the advancement of the symptoms but I did not seem to be getting any better yet. How long would it take this time? Why had I not started to pick up? What did it mean? These and many other such questions flooded my mind.

The numbness did start to decrease, as did the pins and needles but it was not a strong recognisable daily improvement as in the past. I seemed to stay the same with only slight improvements for a long time.

On New Year's Day 2004, Christine came for the day with her children. As ever the boys had a great time with their cousins. I was relieved the boys were really enjoying their Christmas holidays. I still did not have answers as to how long I would be ill, but had now realised that actually there was no Consultant or Doctor who knew the answer. I had learned that each patient with MS is different. The damage to the Spinal Cord can cause a whole host of problems throughout the body. I just really knew about my own condition and that I wanted relief from the intense pain I was in.

Saturday 3rd of January arrived and it felt as though a new attack of MS began. I had increased numbness in my left toes, so much so, I was unable to wiggle or move them at all. The following day the numbness had crept into my foot. However I was able to stand up in

Church and share my Christmas blessings from the Lord, and I enjoyed that.

On Monday 5th January 2004, Peter went back to school and Luke went to my parent's house. The following day he was there again as he started playgroup on Tuesday and Thursday mornings at a Church hall near their home. I am happy to say that he soon loved it there. The following day the strength of the pins and needles had increased. It was advancing from the feet up both legs.

Due to the severity of my condition, my husband worked from home on Wednesday 7th January. We also had to prepare for Luke's 3rd birthday the following day. Thankfully Luke enjoyed his day with us first thing, then my parents came over. They took over the house and cleaned and ironed as well as taking care of Luke and I My parents helped me such a lot that week. I realised how blessed I was to have my parents and family.

On Friday 9th January the school was closed with an Inset day. That meant I had Peter and Luke at home with me and both boys had a Speech Therapy appointment. I knew I could get them both there now on the Mobility Scooter but how would I manage to walk in the Health Centre? I could hardly walk still and yet I could not miss the appointments as we had waited months for the appointments to come through.

When the time came, on the journey there, I had Luke on my knee and Peter sat too, part of the way. Thankfully, I successfully persuaded him to walk some of the way for me, as it was just too painful with two on my knee and a little awkward too. I parked as close as I could to the door of the Health Centre, so there were as few steps as possible to take. I was in survival mode and looked in detail at the premises. It had two entrance doors. The second was a push button access for the disabled. This was awkward, as I could not move quickly enough and Peter had rushed ahead and pressed the button, before I finished getting in through the first door. I remember him rushing through and Luke being unsure about whether to follow and also wanting to press the button himself. He could barely touch it, and so could not press with enough force to operate it, as he was too small. I managed to get there and then somehow lifted Luke sufficiently for him to press the button. He then ran in excitedly to join his brother, whilst I slowly and painfully made it through the second door. I needed someone to find reception for me as I knew there were a limited amount of steps left inside my body. There was no-one there, the waiting room was empty! I vividly remember all of this detail due to the survival mode I was in. Peter did not understand what 'Reception' meant so I encouraged Peter to find people for me and he duly found reception.

There were actually two receptions for different services. Thankfully the one I needed was nearest and I made it, whilst the boys found the toy box I had seen in the distance and pointed out. Once I had made reception aware of our arrival I painfully made progress across to the chairs. I picked a raised high backed chair which would be easier to get out of. The boys played happily until we were called by the Speech Therapist. They even put the toys back into the box when I asked them to. I was of course carrying all the coats by now as well as attempting to walk. I counted each step I made in my head and encouraged myself as I walked down the corridor to the room. This was another such occasion when I wondered if I might faint with the intense pain, but thankfully I did not. I must have looked rough because the Speech Therapist asked me if I was alright and offered to re-book the appointments. I remember thinking that there was no way I had endured so much pain to have to go through it all again! Especially when no-one knew when I would be better, so I just explained it was simply the MS and I could continue with the session.

Luke was seen to first. I had asked for the assessment as I was concerned something might be wrong, as he spoke very little. The Speech Therapist carried out her assessment and I duly found he understood everything that was asked of him. For whatever reason, he had just not developed his speaking skills yet, but he appeared fine. I was so relieved to hear this. He was immediately discharged from Speech Therapy services. That was one less concern to carry around.

Peter went next and whilst he was questioned Luke was happy to do some colouring next to his brother at the table. Peter was learning to recognise his stammer and ways to cope with it. He had many sessions like this one. As he got older, the stammer bothered him more until he was settled in High School. I was told that most children simply grew out of them. Some continued to stammer but learned to handle it, so it was no longer a problem for them. Like the MS there was no quick fix solution to his stammer. The appointments were over and I successfully navigated the way back to the scooter. I thanked the Lord for getting us through what felt like a dangerous experience for me, and getting us safely home again. Later that day Sarah picked up the boys and I and took us to a soft play area for the boys to enjoy in Pontefract.

The next day, my walking had improved overnight. It is a good job as that afternoon we had Luke's birthday party at home. We invited his cousins, family and a couple of friends from playgroup. It was still a physical struggle to make my body move and cope with the pain. I felt very self-conscious every time I stood up and tried to walk. Yet I enjoyed seeing Luke happy, once he got over the shock of having so many people he enjoyed being with, all in our house, at the same time.

On Sunday 11th January, we had a family lunch out with my in-laws. I was beginning to really appreciate these times, which were largely rest times for me. The boys loved the attention of their Nana and Grandad and were less demanding of me. Apart from feeling so self-conscious with the symptoms of MS, I finally realised I enjoyed eating out. It is good not clearing up and washing up afterwards and simply leaving at the end. It finally occurred to me that it did not matter what other people thought of me, although it took some time to absorb that truth. I had to work at it so it still bothered me at times. In the evening I went to the Praise Service at Church which always helped to give me a boost. It was such a happy environment to be in. Even though the constant strong pain made me feel so low, God helped to pick me up through the service.

On Monday 12th January I saw a local GP as my sick note ran out again. The Doctor I saw gave me another note for 2 months. I was walking a little better so this perturbed me a little. Perhaps he was just copying what others had done? Or did he know something I did not know? The questions went on and on in my head as ever.

On Tuesday 13th I awoke to find my walking was not as good. Not only that but I was poorly coordinated and extra clumsy. Was this more of a relapse? What would I do now? By Thursday I had increased numbness in my left foot and left hand. I prayed and Friday saw me able to manage Pontefract with Sarah's help once more. Yet again I found the ever changing symptoms frightening. Sarah was just the calm strengthening presence I needed.

11- The Boys' Baptism

Saturday 17th brought Sheila and Sam from Newcastle. It was a real pleasure to see them. They brought a travel cot for their little one. I was so tired that evening. I clearly remember after putting the children to bed, we were all chatting in the room. We began watching a film and I just had to go to bed. I wondered if I would sleep with the noise of the action film going on downstairs. I was so relieved, it was not a problem for my body.

Sunday 18th January was a wonderful day. It was the boys joint Baptism service at Church. Shelia and Sam were Godparents even though they were not practising Christians, both Mike and I enjoyed them as friends. We felt they would be good roll-models for the boys as they grew up. We also chose Rosie and Jim who were practising Christians. Please note I am saying we chose, as in my husband and I, but I really did the choosing and thankfully my husband agreed. I knew Rosie and Jim would be able to guide the boys in a spiritual sense locally, as they grew up.

I woke up that day and my walking was loads better. A vast improvement overnight! I barely needed the walking stick. I got up at 5:45 and had ten minutes with the Lord before I started making the sandwiches and preparing other food for the buffet after the service. I was a little worried about the time as my husband had to leave with the boys to collect his parents for the service. My husband can be sometimes awkward and unorganised. Thankfully they eventually left with just enough time. Everything else went smoothly. I even managed to rush before I realised just how good my legs were! Sheila noticed and commented on it, which made me feel really blessed.

Some time prior to this the Lord had blessed me with a song called 'Praise Be'. For some reason I had asked to sing this to the Congregation at Church and the Vicar asked me to sing it at the boys Baptism service! I was not and still am not a performer. What was I doing? Yet it somehow seemed right, so I agreed to do so. I was so happy the boys were being baptised. They wore the same gorgeous matching outfits they wore for the wedding in October. They had on matching navy trousers, a light shirt with diamond chequered blue and silvery tie and matching blue and silvery patterned waistcoat. They looked so smart and so cute at the same time. I was so excited, for the very first time with the MS.

The main reading in the service was of the wedding at Cana. This was the same reading my Father had read at our wedding, yet no-one knew that. The Vicar preached on God's goodness, and invited people to come know him personally as Saviour. He explained how He can make all our troubles more bearable and easier to manage.

There were four families including ours there for Baptism's that day. We went up last for the boys to both be baptised. Peter knelt on a chair and leaned over the font to be Baptised. The Vicar asked him to wave at everyone afterwards which he happily did. He received a clap for that. Luke stood up on the chair and leaned over, just as he had seen Peter do. Unlike Peter, he was unable to give his name to the Vicar, so I stepped in. Neither was Luke able to wave at people. I think he was a little overawed by the occasion. I was so proud of the boys!

They returned to their seats and I nervously went to the piano to sing my song. The lady accompanying me on the piano was so good, and she encouraged me before she started to play. I do not know how I managed to sing. The first line was a little shaky, but I improved as I went along. Yet by the end I was not sure I had done it justice. I must have worn my thoughts on my face as the lady at the piano gave me a big hug and said it had been wonderful!

I enjoyed having my friends Sheila and Sam being part of the whole thing, along with Rosie and Jim. Most of my family came too, with their children and I always love family times. The whole service seemed over in no time at all. I thoroughly enjoyed it, and being able to walk so well especially when I realised that the walking was the best since the MS began, and that was just wonderful!

After the service, lots of people came to congratulate Mike and I and tell us how well the boys had behaved. Some also said how my song had touched them. I was told that both my Brother and my Father had shed a tear when I sang. We chatted a while and the boys had their photograph taken with the Vicar and then with family.

We returned home and enjoyed a celebratory lunch. I had invited family and friends back to the house. I had prepared lots of sandwich rolls, my mum brought two large quiches she had made and my husband had bought lots of snacks too and made his delicious 'Tiramisu'. We had a cake for the occasion too. My brother –in-law iced it beautifully! Sheila helped me before and after the service as did my sister Becky and of course my mum. My husband was happy playing host and the children played really well together. The boys received presents from both sets of God-parents and funnily both had bought the same Bible and book of prayers from Marks & Spencer's without knowing this. This was good as it meant both got their own set, so there would be no arguments. The boys had been good friends yet very competitive from an early age.

I lasted all day without my usual afternoon sleep which was unheard of! Although I still had pain with the MS it was significantly less than usual. Subsequently, I thoroughly enjoyed the day, all day long! It was a big rush from start to finish getting up at 5:45 to prepare food. Yet it was a great day and I was overflowing with happiness, a happiness I had not experienced since the MS began. I was sorry when people began to leave later that afternoon. Eventually Sheila and Sam had to leave too to go home to Newcastle, although not until they helped with the clearing up. I knew I had a video of the Baptism service to come, and looked forward to that. I hoped this good day of MS would continue. Perhaps this was the start of my recovery and I could go back to work? I thanked the Lord that day for truly blessing me in so many ways. The future looked brighter.

Monday 19th January rolled around all too quickly and I was delighted my walking was still good and the pins and needles were still less intense too. My husband had arranged to work from home that day. I was very tired after the busy day yesterday but believed I could sleep it off.

Sadly the very next day, I awoke to an increase in pins and needles. The numbness had increased in both feet too and my walking was just not as good. I had a new batch of Physiotherapy sessions at Pontefract Hospital which began that afternoon. Unfortunately, it was when I should have been sleeping in the afternoon. I did not feel as though I could say "No" as they only have a limited amount of appointment slots, and I also needed it to fit within the school day. This was the best that could be achieved at that time. I was blessed by my Father taking me there and back. I was truly exhausted afterwards, but had to keep going, to collect Peter from school and be ready for Luke coming back from my parents' home with my husband, when he finished work. My parents proved invaluable, they had amongst many jobs, taken over the ironing pile with both of them joining in. I found ironing increased the muscle pains in my arms so I stopped ironing altogether and just lived with the creases. Thankfully for the boys, my parents were only too happy to help in this way.

The MS symptoms continued to get worse until Friday 23rd that week. I was back to worrying about what was going to happen next. The fear overtook me. As I write this I see how quickly I went from such a high with the Lord, back to my usual unhappy self. However, I was well enough to go to Pontefract with Sarah, enjoy her company, the Gospel speaker that week, and lunch. I could share all problems with Sarah and she always managed to make them seem smaller and easier to resolve. I could see what a blessing Sarah was to me. I have recorded that I fell down the last two stairs at home that day. Falling always came as such a huge shock over the years. The floor is always surprisingly hard! I had no broken bones, but escaped with bruising. Life continued to rush along with me in tow. I caught flu next, as did my husband so the following week was hard for both of us.

Life rolled on into February 2004 and during this month a man's name kept being brought to me by different people. His name was Joe King. I was told he had a healing ministry in Leeds. I also learned that he was a singer/songwriter and had a number of successful albums.

As a child, my parents had taken all the family to St. Matthias Church in Burley, Leeds, on Sunday evening. My parents taught Sunday School, in a deprived area of Leeds on Sunday mornings. Both enjoyed the teaching on Sunday nights, which helped build them up in their faith. I enjoyed the singing there. It was modern, lively and a happy experience. Joe King had been the worship leader for some of that time. I did not remember him specifically, but reasoned that he must have a good relationship with the Lord.

One of those who asked me to consider asking for his help was my sister Becky. Sarah herself had mentioned his name to me and when she discovered that a number of other people had brought his name to me, she felt I must go and see him. When Sarah rang, she discovered he was not doing individual ministry at that time, but was about to run a 'Healing School' in Leeds. Sarah and I enrolled, as did my sister Becky with a Christian friend of hers. I had little idea of what it would mean, but looked forward with some hope to it beginning on 3rd April that year.

In the meantime life had plenty of Dr's appointments for me or the children and even my husband. On 7th February I had a sudden severe attack of the pins and needles whilst in the supermarket. I found this very frightening. I was on my own looking at clothes when the explosion in my body took place. I did not know if I would faint, or be able to make it back to the car. I wanted someone to rescue me, but there was no-one with me at the time. There were other shoppers but I did not think they would be able to help me and I did not feel able to ask either! I wonder now what a rescue would have looked like? I wanted to be transported in a dignified manner back to the car and I wanted reassurance that the symptoms would pass and things would be ok. This did not happen, but I did manage to safely get back to the car. The violent attack of pins and needles did indeed pass, sadly my fear did not.

On 16th February I went down to half pay! That was a really low time. I had been successful in obtaining Disability Living Allowance (DLA) Even so I now had less income, and the future looked bleak. I had lived through six months of half pay and yet here I was, no nearer to being well enough to go back to work! It was the school Half Term holidays that week too, so I had both boys to take care of, apart from when they were at their grandparents. I felt so frustrated and trapped by my circumstances and the severity of my condition. I quickly applied for Incapacity Benefit.

On Thursday 19th February Occupational Health from work visited me. They explained some alternative possible jobs that could be open to me. It was blatantly obvious to me that I was not capable of doing any work at that time. I was barely coping as it was. Every day was filled with immense pain and walking remained awkward and difficult. I felt as though I had done a marathon every day and was constantly exhausted. I knew if I did not have the children, I would not have wanted to continue living. Occupational Health came up with some possible ideas for when I recovered sufficiently. I just wanted my life back. Yet I wondered if I would get it? Life was simply too frightening.

The next major event was a friend's wedding on 21st February. We attended the wedding and then the evening do at a hotel in Wakefield. I did not want to attend, as I felt so ill, but I pushed myself for my friend. Mandy was every bit the beautiful Bride. She could have no idea how much pain I was in, and I had no intention of telling her. At some point in the evening I needed the toilet, and at this venue, they were downstairs. Sadly, I discovered there was no lift so I had to manage to go down the stairs. I needed two handrails and had to manage with one. How did other Disabled people manage? I wondered yet again. Were there any in the Wakefield area? Or did they simply not go out, due to the lack of suitable facilities? Coming back up the stairs afterwards was even more of a struggle on this occasion. Thankfully my husband was looking out for me by this time and he became the other hand rail for me. I could not wait for the evening to be over. I could not dance at the Disco, I could not go and chose and carry food from the Buffet. I could just sit and watch in pain and I only just managed that. We left at the earliest opportunity. At least I managed to attend for a couple of hours I told myself. I was a mixed bag of emotions and yet I was thankful my husband had brought us, and been there to help me. We had become distant with one another, both trying to cope with my dramatic ill health in our own way.

The following weekend was my husband's birthday. I had caught a bus to Pontefract to buy his present and my nephew's too. 'Just two shops near enough to each other', I told myself. Then I had the frightening experience of feeling faint and wondering if I had enough energy to make it back to the bus stop and get home again. It scared me and yet I was determined to keep going. I believe now in hindsight, that I pushed myself too hard. Yet I also believe that God was watching over me as I always got safely home.

It was my nephew's birthday on the same day as my husband's and he had a party on 28th February. I just had to keep going and going and it felt relentless! I lost my husband in the afternoon to depression. He just laid down on the couch without hope and gave up. I did not want to do that and sought to entertain the boys until it was time to leave for my nephew's party. I felt totally helpless. I could do nothing to help this nightmare end, and so I could do nothing to help my husband. I simply had to continue being mum. Eventually I and the boys persuaded him to get up and we went to my nephew's party. I believe my husband did not come in to the party but looked around a large store instead. He was not coping well. The boys had a wonderful time with their cousins. Once more I felt incredibly alone. When would this time ever come to an end?

We were into March when my body decided it no longer liked Gabapentin. It had not given me any pain relief anyway. I have not recorded the symptoms it gave me, but I usually gave things a good try in order to address the pain issue. I saw the GP on 11th March as my sick note ran out again? It always came around so quickly. The GP I saw this time gave me a sick note for three months! This was the longest time yet and once more I wondered when my recovery was coming and when would I be able to return to work? Frightening thoughts like, "What if I stayed like this?" entered my mind but I refused to dwell on them, as I knew God was going to heal me. I held onto that promise the Lord had made to me with all my might.

12 - Joe King

On Friday 12th March I had the opportunity to join perhaps ten others at a venue in Leeds to join Joe King in worship. I learned he would pray for individuals after the worship. Sarah took me and I was so excited that I would meet him and I would be prayed over. That could be the end of my nightmare! I could be healed! My sister Becky went too with her friend Sue, hoping for some healing of her own. Becky had developed left sided weakness and had some numbness in her legs and feet. What was going on?

The evening was great although the electric guitar would not work. Joe said it had worked fine in the practise ten minutes earlier. He ended up playing the acoustic guitar instead. I really enjoyed it, even though I was painful and tired. I did not know all the songs as some were songs he had composed that I had not heard. Yet all were enjoyable. Afterwards, Joe began to pray for people with a number of helpers. I was initially concerned in case only Joe was anointed.

However it soon became clear that Joe would begin to pray with each person, then leave them with helpers who continued to pray in the same way, whilst he moved on to the next person. Suddenly there was commotion when somebody started shouting in an unsettling manner. I had not been expecting that. Joe explained that the Devil loves to create a commotion and make people afraid, as fear would get in the way of healing. I did my best to ignore the shouting. However, I was not very good at it at all, as I seemed to live in perpetual fear myself.

My sister Becky was prayed for just before me. She began to get vocal about some pain she was experiencing. I don't remember the exact details and neither does she precisely, although she does remember more than I. Suddenly the next noise was that she was healed in Jesus name! Becky began rejoicing and praising the Lord! It was very exciting and the atmosphere was buzzing. When she recalls this event in her life, Becky said she had the overwhelming sense of God's power and presence and was delivered! Her heart was on fire for weeks afterwards filled with His love and joy!

Joe had prayed over me and his helpers continued to pray over me. I remember sharing a little of my personal history, which I found both scary, then liberating once done. There was no apparent change in my condition and yet I felt blessed. It was such a loving environment and it was obvious that those praying, really cared for me and all others who attended. I did my best not to be disappointed, especially when Joe came and spoke to me most gently. He explained that some people don't get healed by the Lord immediately. He stressed the importance of keeping on asking as it said in the Bible (Matthew 7:7)

That day Peter had complained of earache and when I got home he was complaining even more. I gave him children's paracetemol for the pain which was intense. I prayed over him and asked the Lord to heal him. The pain stopped instantly, as suddenly as it had begun as I finished my prayer, so Peter fell asleep and I was able to go to bed myself. In the morning I discovered that Peter had suffered a perforated ear drum. There was a right mess on the pillow case. 'Another job', I moaned in my head and yet I marvelled too, at how quickly God had resolved the situation as soon as I prayed. I really believed it was the Lord, as it had all been instantaneous.

By Monday 15th March, I had another batch of flu with a very dizzy head and this time I could not manage, prompting my husband to take a day's leave from work to take care of us all.

On Thursday 18th March 2004, I finally had a wheelchair assessment. I was determined to go as it had been a long wait since being referred and I had discovered it was good to be able to use a wheelchair for longer trips of walking at shopping centres. It brought an extra piece of freedom. My Father blessed me again, taking me to the assessment centre in Wakefield. It was explained to me that I was not eligible for an electric wheelchair because I was not confined to a chair and could walk short distances. I was eligible for a self-propelled wheelchair only. I pointed out that I could not propel myself more than a metre or perhaps two, due to the muscle pain in my arms, but this made no difference to the outcome. I was measured and told it would take three months before the wheelchair would be ready.

On Friday 19th March I woke up to find that my left hand had gone numb overnight. Not only that, but when I tried to grasp things with it, it gave me a kind of shock which made me feel sick. I found it disturbing that it had happened so suddenly. Yet again I had no idea how long it would last and how I would manage being effectively one handed all of a sudden? What would I do now?

Peter seemed to be mirroring my sicknesses at this time as he got cough after cold after sore throat and so on. We had paid for his first set of ten swimming lessons and it was a waste of money as he was too ill to go. He only managed to attend three out of the ten teaching sessions. I know we are not unusual parents in experiencing this. I learned that School brought a good education and a load of free germs too! Sadly you could not have one without the other.

The following Thursday I saw my Consultant at the hospital. He was always cross and seemed reluctant to do anything. I did not know if there was anything he could do? I wondered what was the point of going? It just seemed to be a case of him logging down my symptoms. I thought that I could tell him those over the telephone. Yet I did not complain to him, just in case he was about to produce some marvellous medicine that would stop the pain and improve the many symptoms. Sadly this was not the case.

By Saturday, I had lost the feeling in my left toes and part of my foot once more. Did that mean I would lose the whole foot or end up in hospital again? I did not know the answer. No one knew the answer. I found it really hard forever living in 'wait and see'. My poor husband found the uncertainty of it all very hard to take too. I had changed and now clung onto my faith with a much greater degree of significance. I did not know if our marriage were to survive? I seemed to be at risk of losing everything I loved.

On Wednesday 31st March the Area Manager of my branch of Housing in Leeds came to visit me with a woman from Personnel. I did not want to see them. I did not want to be what I had become. I could barely stand and it was so difficult to walk. I should have been back at work by now. I knew my poor physical condition would be reported back to my colleagues and I did not want this either. I felt as though I had lost my life, and did not want to be seen. I do not remember what was said, but that kindness was shown. I had received a 'Get Well Soon' card from the office last autumn. It had been signed by all members of the team. Whilst it was good to know they cared about me, it hurt too, as I knew my illness was serious and I just wanted to be back with them.

The next two days the pain of the Crohn's Disease was bad. It was too much to cope with. Yet I knew on

Saturday that the Healing School would begin in Leeds, so I pinned my hopes on that. It was starting on 3rd April and the teaching was to be held fortnightly. I soon learned the point of the course was to teach all attending, how to pray for healing for other people. Somehow I had not quite understood this when I signed up. It soon became apparent that it was very good for me, as I had to stop thinking about myself and the pain I was in, and start to listen to other people.

13 - Healing School

Sarah took me to the Healing School, along with her daughter Louise. We learned of ten possible blockages to healing. They are;

1. Unforgiveness
2. Rejection
3. Previous Involvement In False Religion Occult, Freemasonry.
4. Generational Curses
5. Personal Sin: Worry, fear, guilt, disliking yourself.
6. Sexual Sin – Ungodly Soul Ties.
7. Other Ungodly Soul Ties:
8. Accidents Traumas
9. Demons
10. Negative Binding Words/Self Curses

The first one we looked at was 'Unforgiveness'. The Bible clearly teaches on forgiving one another in the Lord's prayer and specifically in Mark 11:25-26 "But when you are praying, first forgive anyone you are holding a grudge against, so that your Father in heaven will forgive your sins, too." (New Living Translation)

Unforgiveness is very bad for you. We learned that It gives a foothold to the enemy, keeps you trapped at that point, and may allow a disease to take root in your life. At that moment in time, I thought I held nothing against anyone. We learned there is always a consequence to sin, even if it is not seen immediately. There is so much to say about all of these ten areas but to cover this whole piece correctly you really need to find teaching material from Joe King himself. He has a number of books on healing that have been published which give much detail. There are other authors too, but obviously I learned from Joe King.

Personal sin was discussed and the fact that some sins are not recognised as they are socially acceptable, like worry and anxiety. We need to make sure we align ourselves with the truth as in the Bible and seen in Jesus. I recognised myself in the teaching. I realised that I had become very worldly in my views and I knew I needed to change.

Then came a really powerful truth I had never heard before. Proverbs 23:7, "For as He thinks in his heart, so is he." (Amplified Translation of The Bible) This had never been explained to me before. In essence if you think on and believe something, then you will act out that belief in your behaviour. So it was stressed that we needed to make sure we have right healthy thinking, as taught from the Bible and, "We destroy every proud obstacle that keeps people from knowing God. We capture their rebellious thoughts and teach them to obey Christ." 2 Corinthians 10:5 (nlt) If Satan has hold of your thought life, he will be creating negative thoughts causing negative chemical changes in your body, and therefore harming your body. I can remember thinking I had never heard of this before and had no idea how to take captive every thought? How do you do that? I knew I had an awful lot to learn!

We practised our new knowledge on one another, interviewing each other and trying to identify possible problem areas from the interview. I learned that unconfessed sin, is unforgiven sin. Satan loves things to be hidden, in the dark. In this way he can hold onto you leaving you feeling guilty and trapped. Unconfessed sin can cause illness from simple stress and high blood pressure, to something more serious after time. Satan knows the power of forgiveness, so we need to bring every situation into the light. We are saved by the cross, yet we need to seek God and ask for His forgiveness, whatever the situation.

All this was new for me and I found the day both informative and very interesting. I still did not know how to react when there was a commotion of some kind. Someone had been sick on this occasion, and another had done a great deal of coughing. Joe reminded all of us of Satan's tactics in trying to use fear as a hindrance. Yet it was all very 'normal'. There was nothing spooky, no out of body experiences or something so other worldly, as portrayed on some television programmes. We learned how our experiences may have caused us all to make poor decisions at some points in our lives, and these could create a landing strip in our lives for unwanted evil spirits to land. None of us are perfect human beings. We all make mistakes. Yet nothing is too hard for God to sort, as He is the Creator of the entire Universe.

It had been explained that we were in a battle, but that God had won the war through Jesus. However, Satan the enemy, was still doing his best to get in the way and prevent healing and glory being given to God. At that time, I believed the lie that the Devil was equal with God. I saw him as at the opposite end of the spectrum with me and the rest of mankind in the middle. This of course rendered me feeling powerless to do anything.

The Bible clearly teaches that the Devil /Satan is the father of all lies. John 8:44 and in John 10:10 Jesus said, "The thief's purpose is to steal, kill and destroy. My purpose is to give them a rich and satisfying life." (nlt) The Devil is always looking for his next victim. In 1 Peter 5:8 it says, "Stay alert! Watch out for your great enemy, the devil. He prowls around like a roaring lion, looking for someone to devour." I had not received this teaching before, and I was suddenly able to see that I was unwittingly allowing the devil to have a meal out of me on a regular basis. Yet even through that, the amazing thing is that God was still able to use me, to bless someone else!

In one of the exercises, we practiced listening to God. When praying for someone else, we needed to be able to listen for a word from God. We each wrote our name at the top of a piece of paper and then folded the paper twice so that the name could not be read. The papers were all collected and mixed before being handed out. We were then asked to pray for that person, without unfolding the paper and seeing who it was. 'Oh no' I thought to myself. 'What if

I could not hear anything from God for that person?' I along with everyone else, prayed fervently. I did not seem to hear anything at first but then things dropped into my mind. I do not remember exactly what now, but I know I had something encouraging to say to my person at the end of this exercise. A lady found me first and gave me the message she received for me that, "There is hope", she said her verse was based around Psalm 3 especially verses 2-3. I had no idea what this Psalm said and thankfully the lady read my blank look or I said I did not know it. She was able to tell me the verses received from the Lord for me: "So many are saying, 'God will never rescue him! But you, O Lord, are a shield around me; you are my glory, the one who holds my head high." She felt the overriding words for me were, that God would lift me up. Wow! I do not remember ever being prayed for, in such a way with a word someone has received for me. I found myself feeling moved, especially when the lady shared her nerves with me. In spite of her own concerns, she had put herself out on a limb for me.

I looked for my person, who was a middle aged woman. I had received a picture of a healthy tree and rich grass in a garden which looked so inviting, but there was a big building that was somehow in the way for this lady. She was not sure at first, but then thought what it could represent in her life. I did not have a Bible verse to give her and apologised. She was of course kind to me.

Joe then asked us all to say if the word we had received from our person for us, had been accurate? Almost every single one was spot on and blessed the person who had received it. This was amazing given the number of people on the course. Even my woman said she wondered at first, but then realised what it meant and was encouraged, as we all were. So did that actually mean I could hear from God after all? I could not understand God though. How was it that he was able to speak through almost everyone present in order to bless someone? I did not understand, the vastness of this amount of love was too great for me to comprehend. It somehow seemed threatening, although I could not explain why to myself when I thought it over afterwards as there is no threat in love.

It became apparent during the day that the need for total honesty was vital. I realised I needed to be brave and share with whoever would be praying for me that I had been raped by my boyfriend many years ago. Joe knew this as I had shared this with him at the worship evening earlier that year.

When it came for my turn to be prayed for, Joe lead me in a prayer. I have to say that each time I have been prayed over for something painful in my life, I have not been capable of remembering words or prayers to speak out loud. Thankfully Joe said this was common, and Joe led me in prayer line by line. I repeated Joe's prayer he composed for me, based upon the teaching we had that day.

This is the prayer my prayer was based upon; "Lord, I confess that I have not properly loved but I have resented certain people and have unforgiveness in my heart. I repent of this and ask you to forgive me. I call upon you Lord, to help me completely forgive them. I recognise that forgiveness is a decision of my will, not of my feelings. You forgive me whether you feel like it or not. I realise I've been forgiven far more than I will ever have to forgive anyone else. I am extending a forgiveness that they don't deserve, in the same way that I don't deserve forgiveness from you. I'm not letting them off the hook, I'm giving them to you, still wriggling on the hook. I am no longer the judge wanting justice in this situation, wanting what is fair. I recognise that if I want justice for what they have done to me, then the enemy will see that I also will receive justice, what is fair, for all the sins I have committed. I therefore choose to step away from the unprotected place of my unforgiveness into the protected place of your forgiveness.

So I had said it. I had extended undeserved forgiveness to my boyfriend that he did not deserve, just as I did not deserve forgiveness for my sins from God. In doing this I also asked God to forgive me for judging my boyfriend. This meant that I left nothing for the Devil to work on.

At the time, it was hard to say, but I knew that it was exactly what was needed. Prior to this, I had thought I had forgiven, yet I continued to judge my boyfriend, so I certainly had not let him off the hook. I was truly able to let go of him when I prayed, and so cleared away a possible blockage to my healing.

I was also led in a prayer confessing the sin of disliking myself. We all learned to be persistent in prayer, as healing can come 'little by little.' We learned to listen to God whilst praying for another and asking the Lord again for healing if it does not come immediately.

We all had the teaching and then practiced praying over one another. We had to really listen to what each other said, so that you could pray effectively. I realised that although no one else I spoke with was as ill as myself, they all had various ailments or life worries, some of which were significant. I found it difficult to concentrate, but strangely liberating too and I knew it had been a very important day for me.

14 – My Past

The next day 4th April 2004, the degree of numbness in my left hand had increased. The relapse was increasing its strength across the left side of my body. What did that mean? It was now the two week Easter Holidays, so I fixed my attention on the boys. The boys and I spent Monday 5th at my parent's home. My sister Christine was visiting with her children. We all visited Temple Newsam and then a soft play area. The boys had a wonderful time. My parents and my in-laws had both boys that week. I was on my own with the boys on Good Friday only. We visited Mandy and Rupert then Rosie and Jim. Visiting others was a great distraction, so I often visited two particular neighbours on our street. Both showed great interest in myself and the boys, and engaging with them. One of the neighbours had cats, these were really enjoyed by the boys.

My husband had to go into work the following morning and when he came home, I had arranged to see the moving film "Passion of Christ". Mandy took me to see it, although she had already seen it. I had complained that my husband would not go, so she offered to take me. It was a traumatic film to watch. When it was over, my legs would not stand. I don't think Mandy believed me at first , when I spoke the truth. Suddenly I did not know what to do? What do you do when your legs refuse to move? Did this happen to other disabled people? Thankfully my legs soon awoke and reluctantly agreed to slowly leave the cinema. I was so painful but extremely thankful to Mandy for taking me to see this powerful film. She had put herself through the distressing emotions it brought for a second time for me!

On Easter Sunday Sarah collected me and took me to the Daybreak 6am service at the canal. Here with the Vicar and a group of perhaps sixteen others. We sang joyous choruses and read the Resurrection story from the Bible. We all shared barbecued fish which had been slowly cooking during the service. It was a short, but moving informal service. I had not heard of such a service until then. I was so thankful to have been able to go and have Sarah help me to stand on my own two feet. I really enjoyed the service and was deeply moved by the experience. What a vast amount of love for people Jesus had, which he demonstrated by dying for all mankind! I felt so privileged to have been able to attend. I even enjoyed eating the fish. The service had been so moving and I felt I was doing what Jesus had done. I was really happy.

On Easter Monday, my husband, boys and I collected my in-laws and we went for a day trip at Embsay Railway. My mother-in-law struggled to walk with her arthritis. I struggled similarly with the MS, so we both found it hard getting on and off the train. I did not enjoy the fact that I saw I struggled similarly to a pensioner, when I was just 34 years old! My husband noticed too and commented negatively about my progress, which did not help me at all! The boys as ever, enjoyed their Grandparents, just as their Grandparents enjoyed them!

The next day the numbness had begun on the right side of my body. It was in my foot and lower right leg, below the knee. It is such a strange sensation, having partial leg feelings. It makes you keep looking down to see your missing leg or foot. Of course they are always there, however they feel, and they can still carry you with pain as well as with pins and needles.

On Saturday 17th April it was the second Healing School. Joe went through the list he had prepared, of emotional and psychological characteristics people were likely to have, with different medical conditions. He went through a number of conditions and I attempted to jot down as much as possible, but he went too fast for me to keep up. Then he came to Crohn's Disease. I was astonished as he accurately described me and how I behaved. He did not know me and yet everything he said was as if it had been written about me. The previous week, he had asked for people to anonymously write down an illness or symptom they had, for the whole group to pray over. All pieces of paper were collected up and put to one side. Joe had written a list from those papers and based his talk of illnesses and characteristics around that.

At the end of that talk, Joe explained he would pick out an illness/symptom and ask the person who had written it to go to the front to be prayed over. My heart sank as suddenly I knew it was going to be me. I had been practising praying over some of what we had already covered and reading from other sources. All had encouraged honesty with one another, in order to build each other up. All these thoughts came racing into my mind.

The first one Joe picked was from someone suffering from 'Arthritis'. There were approximately 80 people there, but no-one came forward, despite the fact that Joe said there had been three people who had written down 'arthritis'. I knew Joe would pick another, which would be me, and I did not want it to be me. I already felt extremely conspicuous, with the painful stagger walk I did. I did not want to make it worse, trying to stand at the front and sharing something personal. I looked nervously at the floor, childish I know, but it can be effective at times. Joe picked another and read out someone with Crohn's Disease. This was of course what I had written. I held on a moment just in case there was another poor soul with that condition, but no-one moved. I reluctantly made myself get up and go to the front. Little did I know that my mum had been fasting and praying during that week, asking the Lord that it would be me who would be chosen to be prayed over. Looking at the floor had not helped at all!

I was conscious that the session was being recorded for training purposes and did not want a starring role. Yet somehow I knew I was safe, and I felt it was necessary to be honest. I shared a little of a painful piece of my life history, concerning myself and my partner before that time, I will call 'Frank.' He had been an alcoholic which he carefully concealed when we got together. I met him at work. Although I knew he was married, he let me know he would leave his wife for me and I said "yes". You see I was so hurt, having been raped by my previous boyfriend, I was desperate to be loved and accepted.

In order for you to understand, I will explain a little more.

When I was eighteen months old, I needed an operation to unblock the tear ducts to my eyes. The Surgeon at that time, unbeknown to my mother, decided I was too young to remember the experience and therefore proceeded to carry out the operation without anaesthetic! I was held down for the procedure. My mother was told to come back in a couple of hours. When she returned I was very distressed. My mother says I was inconsolable for a few hours afterwards. I subsequently grew up afraid of everybody, except for my mother.

I did not know why I was afraid all the time? As the years passed by, I longed to be like my sisters and brother and enjoy close friendships with others, but I could not do so. I was always afraid of some unknown thing. By the time I reached my teenage years, I realised that nothing bad was actually happening, so I began to push myself and made more friends. Yet I remained essentially a loner. I did not share the usual interests of girls my age, the infatuation with pop stars, make-up and other things I thought were pointless.

I finally bumped into a boy of the same age group at school. Although we shared no lessons at school, we discovered we had the same sense of humour. He also lived in the same part of Leeds so I could easily catch a bus to his home where we enjoyed listening to the 'Top 40' or played board games. It was a relief to find someone to laugh with, after so many years of isolation. When we left school, we kept in contact for quite some time. I think we would still be in contact but I made the mistake of introducing him to Frank. After Frank's death, to me, our relationship became a painful reminder of the past. So I allowed distance to come between us, as I simply did not feel able to handle it.

After 'A' levels, I was tired of education and truly felt I could not read one more book. I did not know what to do with my life. I had initially thought I could be a Physiotherapist, but my grades were not high enough. Neither could I bear the thought of more studying at that time. So I decided to take a year out. My parents saw an advertisement for a job in a Christian hotel in the country. This job would be cleaning, making beds, washing up and so on. Accommodation and meals were free and workers received pocket money and spare time each afternoon. The only negative thing about this job, was that it was in an isolated location. I thought long and hard about it. The countryside is always beautiful and I enjoyed it. I reasoned that it was unlikely anything bad would happen in a Christian hotel. Encouraged by my parents, I applied and was accepted for the post.

My Father took me to my new post. It really was in a beautiful setting. At first, I found it hard fitting into my new community. It was making friends that I found hard as usual, and what do you do after your shift has finished before you are ready to turn in for the night? I remember one such evening shortly after I had arrived, there was a knock on my bedroom door. All staff had their own bedroom. I was invited to a social room with a bar. One of the management team bought me a lager, which I enjoyed. I pushed myself to join in the conversation, and happily found that I settled in after a while and enjoyed myself.

There were two chefs at this hotel, the senior, was a lovely bubbly woman. I had become a vegetarian when I was 17 years old and this Chef, always cooked me a vegetarian alternative, to the main meat dish in the evening. Her junior colleague was a young man my age, amazingly he had been at the same High School as me in Leeds. We had not been in any of the same classes and yet he remembered me, whereas I did not remember him. He told me he once stood up for me when I had been teased by other children. The occasion cannot have been significant to me as I did not remember. He clearly found this annoying, but what could I do? I simply did not remember.

This young man discovered the kind of things that made me laugh and we soon became firm friends. This friendship began to develop into something romantic. It was so exciting to me. I could hardly believe that someone was interested in me? Another older male member of staff from the groundwork team took me quietly to one side. He had seen the start of the romance and warned me saying, "Be careful". "What did that mean?" I asked, but he would not say anything further, but simply reiterated his warning. I quickly dismissed this at the time, as I had fallen head over heels in love by now. Those words came back to my mind after this chapter of my life had finally come to an end. This grounds man clearly saw there was a problem with my boyfriend. I later learned that other women had left suddenly, all of whom stayed in the same bedroom opposite my boyfriend's.

I enjoyed every moment with my boyfriend, and believed he did too. I was eighteen years old and truly believed that we would get married and live happily ever after. When I chose to have sex for the first time with my boyfriend, I was perfectly happy with this choice as we would be together forever. Everybody had sex before marriage, so it was not a problem. At least that is what I believed at the time. I now realise that I had stepped out of the protective covering of the Lord. He will not force His will on us, but allows us free will to choose as we see fit. My poor choice based on a world view, had dire consequences for me. What began as a sweet romance became one of deception, control and manipulation by my boyfriend.

Unknown days past in this loving relationship before things started to go wrong, but I was deeply in love, hook line and sinker. My boyfriend gradually became unavailable on an evening. I did not understand why, but he always gave a reasonable explanation. I mostly stayed in my room waiting for him, just in case he became free. I wanted to spend every possible minute I could with him. This waiting seemed soon to become routine, with my boyfriend suddenly turning up some nights and not others. I would happily have sex with him because our future together was certain in my eyes.

When he was left in charge of the kitchen, he did not provide me with a vegetarian alternative to the meat dish. At first I thought he had simply forgotten, so I was happy to eat vegetables for my main meal of the day. After some time went by, this happened repeatedly and it was noticed and commented on, by one of the management team. My boyfriend had some kind of reasonable explanation that was accepted. It continued to happen every time he was in charge, so I only got a meal with protein if the senior Chef were on duty. I was a little perturbed by this, but not unduly as I was blinded by my love for him.

One day I accompanied my boyfriend to a town to purchase something he required. I do not remember the item, but we went in his car. I was interested in this new town and wanted to explore with him. For some reason he did not want to show me around. I remember talking to him and pausing to look in a shop window whilst still conversing with him. Then he stopped responding and I looked around to find him gone. Where had he gone? Why? I loved him so much, I never wanted to leave him, so how could he have gone somewhere without me?

It then dawned on me that I was in a strange town, with no money or provisions of any kind. I had no means of getting back to the hotel or getting anywhere, except on my own two feet. I did not understand. I waited and passed the time thoroughly looking in this shop window. After approximately twenty-thirty minutes my boyfriend reappeared. He made it clear that I had displeased him by looking in the shop window and he had left me to teach me a lesson. "What!" That did not seem normal behaviour towards the person you loved I thought. As always, my boyfriend had a perfectly reasonable explanation. At least he thought it was perfectly reasonable. He made it seem as though it was me being unreasonable by looking in a shop window. I was not convinced by all of this, but once more whatever the problem was, I felt sure it would be sorted once we were married.

The relationship continued with my boyfriend becoming less and less available. He would turn up late on an evening and after a brief talk he would want sex. I began to become uncomfortable as time went on, because it gradually became apparent that he did not really want to spend time with me. Yet he always had a great explanation, a way of convincing me of his love, without any actual evidence of this, so he would eventually get his own way.

The accusations of infidelity came out of the blue. There was another male member of staff who was the same age I will call Bill. He shared a larger room with another student. They got on like a house on fire and you would often catch them chasing each other and generally playing around like brothers. This made me think of my family. I missed them all and wanted to talk with them, but how could I discuss my relationship with my boyfriend with them? It was troubling me now, but I realised I had no-one to share with. I had been raised in a Christian family and taught to live by Christian principles, which included no pre-marital sex. I knew I had let them down, and just wanted my relationship with my boyfriend to be restored to its happy beginning. I loved him so much. I could not understand why he appeared not to love me anymore in the same way? I can only imagine my boyfriend witnessed me watching this happy scene with the two young men play fighting, or perhaps Bill spoke to me? Whatever it was, my boyfriend suddenly accused me of having an affair with Bill "What?" He said I had been witnessed by an unnamed other, coming out of a hotel room with Bill. I was shocked he could believe such a lie about me. Who would speak such a lie about me? I spoke the truth and explained how I had not even been assigned to that part of the hotel on that day, but had worked in another area, which he could check up on. I had nothing to hide, but whatever I said, he was convinced otherwise.

I now realised that I was out of my depth in this relationship. I loved my boyfriend dearly, but he was changing beyond belief, from the man I first met. I needed to talk to someone, but who? There was no one! My boyfriend always talked the situation around in such a way that made him sound so convincing. But I was unhappy by now, because I could see that he was clearly wrong in his beliefs about me. I did not want to have sex with him any longer and said so. He would argue with me and tell me that he loved me, without giving me any evidence of his love. He tried to make me feel I had actually betrayed him by having what I knew was a non-existent affair with another. He forced himself on me and I would ultimately give up. Perhaps he did love me? Maybe he would go back to the man I loved?

I began to vomit regularly. At first, I and others thought it was a bug. However the sickness persisted. I was still able to work, but eventually one of the management team took me to the Doctors. I was seen by an older male. I do not remember what he said to me, but whatever it was, it did not give me the confidence to share with him exactly what was happening to me. I left with some sachets to restore a healthy electrolyte balance in my body. The one good thing about being sick is that I lost weight. I was a typical teenager, bothered about every imperfection I had, so I did not mind losing weight. It could give me the model figure most women desired, I reasoned with myself.

I was by now very unhappy and felt trapped. My boyfriend did not believe the truth of me no matter what I said. Not only that but he had gradually started saying really negative things to me like, "You'll never amount to anything without me." He spoke lots of negatives over me, and that still stands out now in my memory. He confused me by wanting sex which he said would make everything alright. He would continually come to me with more and more lies he believed about me, and give me more verbal abuse. I just wanted him to stop going on at me, or leave me alone. I was so unhappy as I simply did not understand. He always won the demand for sex no matter what I said. He was the same size as me and yet I could not hold him off mentally or physically. He did not rip the clothes from my body but he did force me to have sex with him against my will, and it happened repeatedly.

My physical sickness continued, as did my weight loss. I was so unhappy and could see no way out of the situation I found myself in. My unhappiness or perhaps the weight loss showed as one evening Bill asked me if I wanted to walk to the local pub for a drink. He was an ordinary friendly type of person and as I was unhappy, I agreed to go with him. We chatted generally on the way there and in the pub. I remember him asking me if I were alright? How could I tell him my boyfriend was demanding sex, being verbally abusive, and believing lies about me having an affair with another. It seemed ironic that here I was, having half a pint with the one man I was accused of cheating with, when nothing of that nature had ever crossed my mind. My love had always been for my boyfriend.

All of a sudden, my boyfriend strode in. He was wearing his Chef's clothes. He stood at the bar waiting to be served. I got up and crossed the room to speak with him. We could have all come down together, had I known he was actually free. My boyfriend then lifted his top discreetly to reveal a long, large, sharp kitchen knife tucked into the waist band of his trousers. He told me that he would sit and drink with us and if he heard anything which he felt was suspicious, and proved his belief that we were having an affair, he would kill him on the spot! I did not doubt his sincerity and was terrified.

I found myself surveying my surroundings, but for what? All three of us sat around this small dark wooden table. We were sat on stools covered in a dark green velvet type material. I was in pleasant surroundings, yet in the most terrifying situation. There were other people in the pub, but it was not full. I wanted to shout for help, but what could I shout and would it make my boyfriend pull out the knife? I sought to make my half pint last. All the time I was waiting, watching my boyfriend, having no idea what I would do if he pulled out the knife. We were there for two whole hours! It was the longest two hours in my life. I remember little of the conversation, just the extremely slow passage of time. I was terrified, which I tried not to show, in case that provoked my boyfriend. A steady amount of people were coming and going throughout this time. It finally came time to leave and we walked together back to the hotel. Only when Bill finally said goodnight and went in, was it over. If there had been any doubts in my head before about my boyfriend, I now knew that he was really dangerous, and I was afraid of what he might do to other people or to me. My boyfriend left me, telling me he still believed the worst of me. If he found any evidence to back this up, he would kill Bill.

I found myself wondering what I should do? I never found an answer. I was so afraid of my boyfriend. He would still continue to turn up demanding sex and lash me with his tongue. I had little fight left in me, I just wanted to escape. I wanted to go home, but I had insufficient money to pay for transport and what on earth could I tell my parents on my return? I felt like a caged animal.

One afternoon during time off, I went for a long walk into the countryside. I just walked and walked and then it began raining hard. I kept going and darkness began to fall. The weather began to get wild. Suddenly I ran into some walkers, coming down the path in the direction I was headed. They were professionally dressed in walking boots and rain gear. There I was in my trainers and insufficient jacket. I was soaked to the skin, and it didn't matter to me anymore. I was just going to continue going forward but one of the women grabbed my arm and stopped me. "You're not going out there are you", she asked? "It's too wild, too dangerous!" This was a complete stranger, but I was moved by her compassion for me. She shocked me out of the mind set I had and I found myself replying "No, I was just walking". She left with her two companions. I did not know her, yet she stopped me in my tracks and today I am thankful that she did so, and would advise anyone else to always act as she did. I think God motivated her to save my life that day, as I would have taken that dangerous path in stormy weather if not for her.

Now I had been stopped in my tracks I suddenly came out of the fixed mentality I had been in. I wondered what I should do? The reality of my situation hit home. I was stumbling around as it was now dark and I was cold and soaking wet. The need for shelter and warmth overcame all other desires. I knew I had nowhere to go and so set off back to the hotel, with my heart in my boots.

On my return I discovered concern had been raised for my welfare. Mountain Rescue had been called out, and were looking for me at that time. I felt bad at that point, as I knew what a great job mountain rescue did, saving lives for those who had suffered an accident whilst out walking. Here I was having gone walking in trainers. I needed rescuing, but I did not think it was the type of rescue they could perform. The lady in charge ran me a hot bath and someone went to my room to collect some clean clothes. I had no idea what to do next, I felt like I was drowning.

I made it to bed and all too soon it was the next day and life continued. I had no idea what I said to those in authority when I was questioned. My boyfriend had told them that I was having an affair with another and he was believed! There was no doubt he had a silver tongue. It did not matter what I said, he had covered his tracks well and management were deceived. I did my best to carry out my duties as normal. The vomiting continued and my boyfriend remained in control.

Time rolled on and another day I decided to walk to a new town. It took me two hours! There I bought a bottle of white wine. My parents had not drunk wine at home. I think I associated it with parties and celebrations yet I did not know what it really tasted like? I bought it, as somehow it seemed luxurious and lovely, I began exploring in the town and looking around in the shops. Suddenly I bumped into some of the hotel management. There was no way I could have walked back in time for the evening shift by then. I do not know how I would have got back either, I had not thought that far ahead, it was as though a part of me had just given up. They gave me a lift back to the hotel.

Another afternoon I had a persistent headache, so I had two paracetamol. I suddenly remembered that I had bought this bottle of wine and decided to have a glass. I remember being disappointed as it did not taste as pleasant as I thought it would. Yet it was not truly horrid so I drank it. A short time later, within the four hours you should space paracetamol, I still had the headache. So I took two more paracetamol and drank another glass of wine. As time passed by I drank more wine and had more paracetamol. I did not realise the harm I was doing to myself. I just wanted the headache to go away. I wanted to escape and sleep peacefully.

I did not turn up for the evening shift. I awoke to the banging on my bedroom door. How long I had been unconscious I do not know? When the consumption of wine and 13 paracetemol were discovered, I was rushed to the nearest ' Accident and Emergency Unit' where I was to have my stomach pumped. I had drifted in and out of consciousness on the journey there. My boyfriend had insisted on coming. I overheard him telling the man concerned of my volatile unstable mental state. There truly was no escape from this man. Perhaps I would be able to tell someone at the hospital.

I had some bloods taken on arrival at the hospital swiftly followed by having my stomach pumped. The tube that you have to swallow, makes it feel as though you cannot breath. The liquid that is flushed down makes you vomit again and again. Yet the nursing staff continued pouring more liquid down. Eventually it was finally over. I was left exhausted in the room with one nurse who was cleaning up. I was no sooner alone with her than she started to shout at me for being an attention seeking, spoilt child. I feel sorry for this nurse now. She would have felt terrible if she knew the truth. She could have tipped me over the edge, but instead I found myself wondering what could be going on in her life to cause her to behave so inappropriately? She knew absolutely nothing of me, other than what she saw, or perhaps she heard a lie from my boyfriend? I hope she did not practice this pattern of behaviour again on another innocent victim.

I was left to wait, attended by another nurse. Finally news came that the blood tests taken were all clear and I could go home. I went back to the car with my boyfriend and the man from the management team.

Once in the back of the car again I found myself drifting into sleep. Not before this man voiced his concern for me. This was quickly suppressed by my boyfriend and I did not hear anymore until we arrived. My boyfriend escorted me to my room, privately telling me he had told Management all about me and whatever I told them, I would never be believed. 'What did that mean he had made up now?' I thought to myself and yet I knew it no longer mattered, as I felt numb inside. The last time he had demanded sex, I had physically managed to hold him off. I did not care anymore if he had a knife on his person and would kill me, it was as though something inside of me had snapped and died. Now back in my room as he threatened me some more, I resigned myself to my fate. I was so lost. All fight had gone.

The next day I did not start work as usual, but had breakfast and then went to the Managers office. He asked me questions and they were filled with assumptions based on the many lies my boyfriend had told him. I actually feel sorry for the management team there at that time now. They truly had no idea what was going on. My boyfriend was so deceitful, cunning and manipulative, he really had a gift for making himself believable. There I was at eighteen years of age, with no such skill and no idea how to deal with someone who did?

I could tell by whatever was said, that those in charge were concerned for me even though they believed my boyfriend's lies. It had been decided that I must return home. My parents had already been rung and told the shocking news about my condition. He rang my mother right then, as she wanted to speak with me. I hated that, I knew my poor mother would be so worried about me. Her concern came across on the phone. Yet I knew I could not share what had happened with her. When I put the phone down, the man told me that I would be taken home by my boyfriend. So the torture had still not finished! I packed my clothes and left with my captor.

On the journey to my home at times I felt my boyfriend showed some compassion towards me. However, this was soon lost when he warned me not to tell anyone, as no-one would believe me, he had made sure of that. He reinforced his manipulation by refusing to stop on the journey for a toilet break. I was in a lot of pain by the time he finally relented. I did not understand what had happened to him. Where had the man gone I fell in love with? When we finally reached my parent's home in Leeds, he came and opened the car door for me and I suddenly saw a spark of who he had once been and gave my captor a kiss. What was I doing? When would this end? He did not stay, other than to hand me over officially as per the instructions from the hotel. I wondered if it were finally all over?

I was so shocked when I was back at home and I realised all that had taken place, had happened in just one calendar month's time! One month! It felt like a whole year's amount of events to me. Just one month to lose almost two stones in weight. Just one month to change my life for worse, to make me a total wreck! That was all it took – one month!

My parents were shocked and disappointed by what had happened. I do not think I was able to give them an adequate explanation. I do not remember what I was able to share. I just know I was unable to share the truth about my boyfriend. I remember having to see my local GP. My mother worked in that Doctor's Practice as the 'Sister'. The Doctor was a lovely older chap who treated me with great kindness. He explained physiologically what I had done to my body and asked me why? Of course I could not tell him, but I did explain that I had not intentionally decided to commit suicide. He asked me to promise that I would never do it again and I promised. The vomiting stopped as soon as I was home, although I did not understand why. My mother immediately set about building me up.

As time went on, my former boyfriend would call me on the telephone. I thought I had escaped and yet here he was threatening me over the telephone. His manipulation continued. Always he spoke unkindly and painted a bleak picture of who he believed I was. Always, he warned me never to speak of what had happened, because I would not be believed. He spoke of how I was despised by those I had worked with and I could not understand him. I found it distressing because I was powerless!

One day my mother arrived home when I was crying, after the end of one such telephone call. At the time I wondered if there was truly was escape from him? My mother of course asked why I was crying and I managed to say about his unkindness to me in that phone call. My mother immediately rang the hotel and let it be known, in no uncertain terms, that man was never to ring me again. She was so angry, she managed to permanently sever the link. I was so relieved it was finally over! He never called again.

I was devastated by the whole experience and felt so guilty that I had not kept to my Christian values. I had pleased myself and had lost my virginity, believing the lie that we would marry and live happily ever after. I felt so foolish and cheap. I had hurt my parents too even though they did not know it. How could I have made such a terrible mistake? What did God think? Did He still love me? Why didn't He stop me somehow? Yet I knew I had made that initial decision, no one made it for me. But still, I felt abandoned by God.

Now as I look back I see God did not abandon me. That was a lie from Satan, who loves things to be hidden in the dark. I had stepped away from God by choosing to do my own thing. The Lord warned me through the grounds man, who obviously suspected the truth about my boyfriend. He showed his compassion for me through Bill, who tried to get me to confide in him twice. The Lord protected me when I was walking in wild weather in the dark, through the concern of a stranger. He sent Mountain Rescue out to find me. He even stopped the combination of wine and paracetamol from killing me! God showed me that the Management team cared for me, they were simply truly deceived themselves by my boyfriend. I felt alone at the time, but as I look back now, I see Gods hand at work. Although I had effectively stepped back from the Lord, He had never stepped back from me.

The rape left me feeling so dirty, as this experience does. At the time I felt there was no-one I could share it with. I attempted to bury this painful chapter of my life and subsequently began a three year severe depression.

15 – Frank

It was over four years later in my first full time job,
I had been flattered by Frank's attention at work.
He made me laugh and made me feel there must
be something good about me after all. Sadly he was
married but this was not the end, as he told me he
would leave his wife for me. I was so hurt inside from
the rape, I said "Yes". We moved into a flat of our own.
His secret alcoholism became evident over a period of
time. He wanted to stop drinking but was unable to
achieve it. I loved him so much, I thought I could help,
if I just loved him a little more and tried a little harder.

I introduced him to the Lord Jesus. We attended a
Methodist Church together and Frank enjoyed the
teaching and being 'confirmed' there. He enjoyed
knowing he was loved and accepted by the Lord just
as he was. His new faith gave him a sense of hope to
hang onto throughout the rough times.

We were together for two years and the relationship
was wonderful, until the alcoholism eventually took

complete hold of Frank. I would find cans and bottles hidden in the flat, even in the toilet cistern! I eventually left when he became violent, although he did not manage to hurt me. He was always broken after he had tried to hurt me, and I felt his pain keenly.

Just one occasion stands out in my memory. At that time, I just knew there was a bottle of spirits hidden in a certain cupboard. He tried to deny it was there, but I just knew without a shadow of a doubt. He realised he had been caught out. Suddenly a change came over him. It was as if in his head, I had become his jailer. I was reaching up into this cupboard to grasp the hidden bottle that I still had not seen, when suddenly he grabbed me back aggressively, and turned me, pinning me against the louvre, slatted wooden door. His fist was rushing through the air towards my face and amazingly everything went into slow motion. "How had this happened?" I thought to myself. "This was something you saw in a soap opera, not something in my life. Yet there it was, the fist was coming towards me to hit me in the face and it would hurt." I do not know how I managed it, but I thought all of that and dodged at the last moment and his fist went through the door! The noise seemed incredibly loud, as the wood shattered into pieces and fell to the floor! I ran straight to the flat door and ran out and down the stairs to the next level, where there were entrance doors to two other flats. I left the door open and waited a little while. I knew he would not be able to follow me down, whilst he was angry or broken. I knew I would be safe, as there were other people in those flats. After a while, I went back up to the flat and found him crying. He was truly sorry, but this time I knew for certain that he would hurt me, if I remained. I told him to contact me, when he stopped drinking. I packed a bag and left to stay with one of my sisters.

As I look back at that incident I am certain that the Lord slowed time down for me, enabling me to think and move at the last moment, escaping unharmed. In fact, I think God put me just out of reach every single time Frank lashed out, and threw something at me. I moved or he missed every single time. I was never hurt, which is amazing!

I remained in contact with Frank via the telephone, as I still loved him so much. He left the flat and went to live at his Father's home. My heart was tormented as I wanted him back so much! He made many promises to me to stop drinking, but he did not stop drinking. Every so often we would meet up and hold each other again, as we missed each other so much. Every time, Frank would make promises to me about stopping drinking. Sadly, he was not able to keep them, so I gradually saw him less and less.

Frank made a new group of friends he met in a pub. He told me about this group he spent money on. Frank had acquired money from the divorce settlement he had with his wife. I do not know how much this amount was, but his new friends discovered he had money and persuaded Frank to buy a second hand car for them, occasional drugs and other things. I was worried these people were up to no good, when Frank shared this with me. However, he was convinced they were his friends. Finally one day, some months after we parted company, we met in Leeds city centre for the last time. He shared with me his concerns that they had spent thousands of pounds of his money, and he would have nothing left if it continued. He was clearly troubled so I advised him to go to the Police. He was horrified at this suggestion at first, as he really saw them as friends. I pointed out that if they really were true friends, then he could say to them that he did not want to spend any more money, and they would be fine with that. If that was not the case then he should go to the Police. That was the last time I ever saw him.

I spoke with Frank on the telephone, after he had told his friends he was not happy to spend any more of his money on them. I do not know exactly what their response was but it was not positive and Frank felt they were trying to pressurise him, so much so, he did indeed go to the Police. One of the group was questioned by the Police, I do not know which one. The ring leader of this trio of men found out, and they turned up at Frank's Father's home. They managed to drug his Father by slipping something in his tea. He was unconscious for twenty-four hours. The three men cruelly tortured Frank, before killing him.

At this time, I had found love again, sadly with another married man. I missed the shocking news on the television and in the newspapers, as I had gone away with my new boyfriend for the first time that weekend. I was devastated at the news when I returned to my sisters' home. I had stopped being in love with Frank, but cared deeply for him. My new love, was both a perfect gentleman and tower of strength helping me through that time. I am happy to say after some years we married and remain so.

What happened to Frank really disturbed me. I felt my life was way out of control, in spite of my new love. It all seemed too much. After some months of feeling utterly shocked, pained by and partly responsible for Franks' death, it suddenly came to me, that there was one thing I could be in control of in my life. I could control the amount of food I ate. This meant that after my boyfriend and I set up home together, I would disappear after tea each night and make myself sick, in order to be in control. Of course I was soon 'bulimic' and not in control at all.

16 – The First Healing

I did not tell of the rape or give quite this much detail of Frank at the Healing Conference. I explained about the relationship, his alcoholism, our parting and his murder, for which I felt partly responsible. When I told them of Frank's murder a gasp of horror went up around the room. It was so difficult expressing my personal life to the people there. Yet as I opened up, the other attendees gave me their non-communicated support. I stood with Joe King, who was equally shocked and had to think quickly on his feet, as he continued to lead. I am sure he will have sent up lots of "Help" prayers of his own, at that point. It was frightening, but it was all true and I had a small sense of relief once I had shared openly.

Joe asked me a few questions to clarify what I had shared. Then he asked if anyone knew the root of Crohn's Disease, which is an autoimmune illness. One man shouted the correct answer, which was 'self-hatred'. Joe then asked me if I thought I had low self-esteem and if I had a difficult child-hood? I said 'yes' and explained about the Surgeon who operated on me when I was just 18 months old. He decided I would be too young to remember anything, and insisted on giving me the operation without anaesthetic. I subsequently grew up afraid of everyone except my mother. I used to get cross with myself for not making close friends and going and doing things, like my sisters and brother. But I couldn't do them, because I was too afraid of people.

Joe anointed me with oil and asked for other members of his team including Sarah, to come and pray with him over me. This is what I remember from the event. Joe began by binding any spirits from interfering with the process. I tried to relax as instructed and he prayed for a fresh anointing of the Holy Spirit to fill me. I tried hard to concentrate on breathing in and mentally pictured myself drinking from a cup full of the Holy Spirit. I had to tell my thought life to shut up, and really focus on drinking from the cup in my head.

First I was led in a prayer to forgive the Surgeon, which I repeated phrase by phrase, based on the forgiveness prayer we covered the previous session. I was led further to forgive those responsible for Frank's murder. Joe led me in a prayer renouncing the self-curses I had given to myself over the years. This had created a landing strip, giving permission for spirits of infirmity to land in my life. Joe kept praying for more Holy Spirit and asking me to breathe it in. He commanded any spirits of self -hatred that had come into my life on the back of these events, to leave me at that moment. I was encouraged to cough or breathe anything out. Joe and helpers were gathered around me praying now and the power and presence of the Lord was so strong. As the praying continued I felt myself swaying and heard someone say that it was safe to fall. So I let go of all inhibitions and was safely caught on my way to the floor. The group continued to pray over me, at some point they had begun to pray specifically for the Crohn's to be healed.

I was encouraged to hand over 'Frank' to the Lord. I pictured Frank in heaven, I took his hand which I was holding onto, and gave it to Jesus and let go. Frank was happy and smiling and then he melted away with Jesus and was gone. I was both happy and sad in that moment. I had effectively said goodbye to Frank and that chapter of my life. Then I felt such an enormous deep sense of peace. I knew immediately that I had been healed of Crohn's Disease. I felt different in my core. There had been some kind of major seismic shift within me, and I felt truly blessed! I still had the fire burning in my abdomen that was always present with the Crohn's Disease, yet I knew without a doubt that I was completely healed!

Once the Crohn's Disease had left, the opposite blessings had been prayed into me. Instead of self-hatred, self-love and the love of the Lord was prayed into me. I learned this as always the case once something is evicted, the opposite blessing is prayed in, in its place. This prevents the spirits re-entry. The person is then protected unless they step back into their old ways of self-cursing, or whatever un-biblical practice added to their downfall. All those wonderful words spoken over me went around and around in my head, and I stayed extremely happy and peaceful for the rest of the day.

Later that evening back at home, from that night on, I never woke again in agony in the middle of the night with abdominal pain. The fire in my abdomen began to decrease in strength, over the next three months until it went out and away completely. Satan did try to give me symptoms a few times during this period, but they did not fit in with the usual pattern of Crohn's Disease. Joe had warned me it was possible this may happen and to stand my ground and declare my healing from the Lord. Each time that happened, I stood my ground on my healing by the Lord and declared it out loud. I refused to have these false symptoms or dwell on them. I dwelt on God's healing touch instead. I spoke out loud, verbally declaring what He had done for me at the Conference, and I praised the Lord. So each time the false symptoms left, and I have remained healed since! I have found that the devil is a persistent liar and trouble maker, but God's love is more powerful. Praising Him, makes the devil leave in the end, as he cannot stand to hear the worship.

I have no food restrictions as I did with the Crohn's Disease and do not look at food and wonder how much pain it could cause me later on in the night. This was an enormous blessing after 12 years of pain! I knew that my God loved me! I was truly amazed at this wonderful experience. After that, I received teaching on learning to love myself, to read scriptures on how much God loves me. Taking it all like daily medicine, in order to build myself up.

17 – Back to Earth & Deliverance

In the early evening that same day, my eldest Cousin and his partner came up from London. They were supposed to visit in the autumn, but I had been in hospital with the MS. It made me sad when I realised the MS was hardly any better at all. I tried to hang on to my experience, yet having guests meant having questions, these brought home the miserable stark reality of the MS. My cousin and now wife, are a lovely couple who were both supportive, and great fun with the boys too. It felt as though they bought a little sunshine with them. On the Sunday we all took the boys to a nearby children's adventure park. The boys had a wonderful time and we really enjoyed their company and their love. Later on in the afternoon, we saw them back to their train to London. It was and is so good, to spend time with supportive family.

On Thursday 29th April, my husband invited me to go to a Jazz concert with him. He was finding our wobbly relationship situation uncomfortable too, and was trying to make things work as best he could. I did not like going out anymore on an evening as I was simply too tired and felt ill all the time. That made it difficult to concentrate on anything. I too however, wanted to make our marriage work and so I agreed to go. One of our kind neighbours babysat for the boys. We went to the Leeds College of Music to see the Duke Ellington Jazz Concert. I don't remember great detail about the performance, except that I enjoyed the big band sound in spite of the pain. I am thankful both my husband and I were committed to our relationship. I have learned over the years that sadly half of husbands/partners leave on the others diagnosis of MS, so I am truly blessed my husband has stood by me.

On 1st May it was the third Healing School'. Sarah took me to another day of studying and prayer. We carried on our practice of listening to God exercises. This time I got a picture of a child on a swing in a garden. I could hear children's laughter. The garden was beautiful and a bush was full of pink blossom. It was not manicured, but it was beautiful and I had a strong sense that it was safe. This turned out to be a message for a chap who had no idea what it meant and was quite adamant it must be incorrect. I did my best not to be disappointed. Later however, another was praying for him, again without knowing it was him. I heard afterwards this lady had a picture of this chap as a puppet on strings, with a feeling of weightlessness. She felt the Lord was saying that he was completely safe with Him. The chap mentioned the swing picture I had given and the woman said how it fitted perfectly, as on a swing, you are not supporting your own weight either. I was so relieved! God is amazing!

I was blessed when I prayed for another that day. Once more I did not know whom. It turned out to be a message for a middle aged man. I prayed and I felt this man was struggling. I also got a verse from the Old Testament and I was embarrassed I did not know exactly where it came from? However, when I shared with the man concerned the gist of the verse, he knew it immediately as Isaiah 43:2. "When you go through deep waters, I will be with you. When you go through rivers of difficulty, you will not drown. When you walk through the fire of oppression, you will not be burned up; the flames will not consume you." He explained carefully, whilst working on maintaining his composure. It fitted perfectly, as his father had died recently, and he had found it so hard to deal with everything concerned. Those Bible verses meant a lot to him, and had even been part of his father's favourite hymn. Wow! That hit me, I felt I knew so little, and yet God could still use me to bless someone else!

At the end of this day I spoke with Joe about my Son Peter, who was troubled with persistent nightmares at that time. He questioned me about Peter and asked me to compose two prayers, one to pray with him and one to pray over him with others. From my records he encouraged me to pray with Peter asking him to pray and verbally give his fear to God and instead think on God's goodness. He advised, that I write a prayer based on the teaching we had on the course. This was including binding any spirit's from interfering in that ministry in Jesus name. I needed to thank the Lord for Peter, for being there right from his conception, to this day. Also to thank Him for His love for Peter, that He would never reject him, and other such wonderful truths from the Bible.

Peter's birth had been particularly difficult, so I specifically prepared prayer over the fear of death in us both at that time, from the teaching notes. I thanked the Lord that Peter was loveable when he came into the world and nothing had changed. I included a sentence commanding all evil spirits to leave and the opposite good things to be prayed into Peter.

I am glad I made hurried notes before we left the Healing School as there was a lot to remember. I felt a great sense of urgency to do this, and so I worked hard on this at home in the evening and prayed with Peter, before he went to bed that night as advised.

I worked hard on composing the prayer to pray at Church over Peter the very next day, to say with two individuals I chose, and felt would be suitable. I rang them that evening and both agreed to pray the prayer over Peter. Time felt crucial in this matter and so I asked the two individuals to pray with me over Peter, immediately after the Church service, just giving them the prayer to read immediately before we prayed. I read through the prayer with them both, and Peter responded verbally as appropriate. He was able to verbally announce that he wanted no more fear and nightmares. I was able to command any spirits to leave, and Peter acted with relief and happiness. I prayed for all empty spaces in Peter to be filled with God's Spirit, confidence and a strong sense of God's love for him. I thanked the Lord for all He had done and would continue to do. Peter was so happy to have been prayed over and appeared to feel really blessed!

He had no more nightmares at that time and for some time afterwards! I was so happy myself, I really felt God had answered our prayers!

Unfortunately, the two people I had prayed with, had felt uncomfortable with the prayer. They were not used to such praying and raised their concerns with the Vicar. He in turn another day, possibly the next Sunday, spoke with me. He was one of many Christians who do not like the 'deliverance' ministry. I made sure I subsequently kept all the teaching I had, between Sarah and myself from that time on, out of respect for the Vicar. He had blessed me a great deal making it possible for me to take Alfie to school, by taking Alfie Lyle and I to school for six weeks. I did not understand why he could be against deliverance when Jesus did it? Yet I had no desire to upset him. I learned that some Christians do not like deliverance because it is messy, both physically and emotionally. It can involve people shouting, screaming, crying, coughing, being sick and generally means having to deal with the unexpected. Some people fear losing control, or being ill-equipped to deal with all of the above scenarios.

18 – The Rollercoaster Continues

On 3rd May 2004, I woke to find the pins and needles had increased greatly in strength in the right hand side of my body. They were stronger in my foot and up into my leg and knee. I did not realise the true extent of this until I got out of bed and began walking. I hated waking up to dramatic changes like this, it was always such a shock and I found it frightening. I did not want this relapse to end in hospital admission. I also had soreness in my bladder and I worried about what was going to happen next?

By Wednesday 5th, the soreness was worse and I had lower back pain on the right hand side of my body, along with a dizzy head.

I rang and made a Doctor's appointment for the following day. I was examined and treated with antibiotics for a water/kidney infection. Throughout this week I continued to take and collect Peter from school. I prayed God would give me strength and see me through it, with all the extra symptoms and He did!

On Monday 10th May I was feeling a little better and it was a good job as I had an appointment with the Beta-Interferon Consultant. My thoughts about having this self-injected treatment and young children in the house had not changed. Neither had my views on looking after young children whilst suffering flu-like symptoms. He pointed out that some only have symptoms for 24 hours. Yet I knew that some have symptoms for longer. I did not want an increase in any symptoms, on top of the amount of pain I was already enduring. I may have thought differently if we did not have the boys, but we did, so I agreed only to think more about it, as he was such a pleasant man, who seemed genuinely to want the best for me.

The next day I came down with a sickness bug and the runs, or D&V as it had always been called by my parents. I was up most of Tuesday night and into Wednesday. The sickness was so bad that I chose to fast all day Wednesday.

On Thursday the MS symptoms had become significantly worse. The pins and needles had increased in strength and had moved up into my back.

It was worse in my arms and legs and I had a new site of them in my head. Was nowhere exempt? I thought I had them everywhere in the past, but did not remember them being in my head. In spite of all this, I was still able to take Peter to and from school and see to Luke. God supplied the strength I needed to get through each and every day.

I learned that the MS symptoms always became worse when there was another illness added. If ever I did without a meal, this was reflected in worsening symptoms too. I would like to say I realised this immediately, but it took me some time.

On Saturday 15th May I had recovered enough to attend the final 'Healing School' in Leeds. I enjoyed it as ever. The teaching continued on learning how to pray for others. We practised leading people to forgive others, God and themselves as appropriate. The power of forgiveness in this prayer really struck me, and brought home the truth that no-one deserves it. I realised I needed to hand all of my past over to the Lord, as I could see that I had not completely done so. I needed to forgive all who had once hurt me and no longer judge any of them.

At the end of the day one of the prayer helpers came to me and asked to pray over me. She prayed that I would be able to use my suffering to help others who have suffered, to ease their pain. She anointed my lips, so that I would speak the words of Jesus and be a real blessing. That people would be able to come to me, knowing I would pray for them. The woman prayed that I could help them and make a positive difference in their life. She asked God to anoint me doubly and after she had prayed, said she felt God would use me mightily. When I came to read the notes I had made at the time of the 'Healing School, I was amazed, when I read this. I did not remember this prayer time, until I re-read the notes I made. God is so amazing, as I can see He has been using me to do exactly what this woman prayed!

It was about this time when Louise came to speak to me. She had received a word from the Lord for me. I wondered what it would be? The Lord had told her to pass on a message which was; "Do not worry about the songs. The Lord was going to bring out the songs at a future time to bless others at just the right time." I had been worrying about the songs God had blessed me with since the MS began as I knew they would bless people in need. I was not a performer and wondered how God would see to it. Now I knew He had the situation already in hand, so I was able to let go of it and leave it with Him.

On the final day, we did not manage to finish the teaching so an extra session on the following Saturday evening was arranged. I did not like doing anything on an evening as I was so tired and painful. Yet I wanted to finish the teaching we had received, as I knew it might be useful one day. God had blessed me by healing the Crohn's Disease and healing Peter of nightmares. I consequently felt like I wanted to do it for Him, so decided that I would definitely attend.

Sunday 16th arrived and at 3.30 am Luke began being sick. The poor lad was sick lots and I had to see to him as my husband was getting up to go to work at his Sunday job. Luke continued to be sick into the next day and I managed to get him in to see the Doctor the day after that. Of course the Doctor was only able to give sachets to readdress the electrolyte imbalance in his body. My mother came the next day and took care of Luke to give me a break, and I needed it. I also had a B12 injection due. Since having Luke my body never recovered the ability to store iron and I had been consistently anaemic. These injections gave me a much needed boost. They helped me feel less breathless, which I always felt by the time the injection was due, and less exhausted too. I needed every boost I could get. The injection is more painful than others, because I am told it uses alcohol as it's carrying agent and has to go deep into the muscle. You could choose to have it in your backside or in your arm. At first they put it in my rear, but aside from the indignity, this made no sense to me because you then sit down and it throbs more due to sitting on the site of what your body sees as an injury. I found it so much better when I asked to have it in my upper arm near the shoulder. At least this way you could choose to rest the arm a little afterwards and not squash it.

Luke gradually recovered from the sickness bug and just as he did so, Peter caught it. I was so glad my husband was able to get up during the night to see to either of the boys. I was in so much pain and sometimes I was so exhausted, I did not even hear them. Once again God met my needs.

Peter recovered more quickly than his brother and so I was able to take them both to Church on Sunday morning. I found Church a real source of strength by this time. It built up my faith and my friends from my House Group encouraged me, as did other members of the Congregation. I learned over time that if I missed it, I missed out. I had been for some time on a rota, as part of the 'Welcoming Team.' In this role I welcomed all who came at the beginning of each service and hugged where appropriate. I thought about the needs of others, instead of my own. Once more it was good for me to escape my tormenting thought life.

On Monday 24th May, I had an appointment to see my Consultant at Pinderfield's Hospital. My Father took me to this appointment and I have logged in my diary that it was OK. That means my Consultant must have finally changed in his attitude towards me. The change came whereby he would get up out of his seat when I entered the room, and he would smile and shake my hand! He asked me how I was, as though he cared. I had always enjoyed this in Leeds at the Crohn's clinic, but never before with my Consultant for the MS. It was a pleasant change and was the end of all hostilities. I was so relieved, as at the time I was not able to understand what the problem was with the Consultant? In hind sight, I am sure he had undergone a disciplinary procedure and training by now. A direct result of whoever formally complained. I do not know if they realise what a positive effect they had on that man, and in turn on me. I will always be thankful to them.

The week went on and with help from Grandparents once more, I had the boys on my own just two days that week. I planned painting, playdough and other activities and took them to the park with Luke on my knee on the Mobility Scooter. Then usually after I had made lunch they chose a children's film to watch whilst I slept. There was just one more activity to plan, often a board game, before children's television began and after that, my husband arrived back from work. The boys were always so excited about their Dad returning from work and would inevitably want to watch for his arrival at the living room window. We used to have a couch underneath the window. I loved watching them run across the room and throw themselves onto the couch with such gusto. They would then jump and jiggle about excitedly often getting up and down again and again until, "Dad's home!" They would both rush to the door and fling themselves at their Dad, who was equally overjoyed to see them and receive such a rapturous welcome! The Pain and exhaustion were terrible and yet the moments of happiness like these were so precious! I just wanted to sit and rest then until tea was ready, but there was invariably some cleaning up to do. I would allow myself a short break and then force my painful body to get on with the necessary jobs, whatever they were.

My husband is a great cook and we all enjoy his meals. I would find that approximately twenty minutes after the meal, I would get a new surge of energy, ready for the next chapter of the day which was washing up and making my husband's sandwiches for the next day. Bath time swiftly followed, then the bedtime stories. Luke was in bed first then Peter. By this time it had gone 8pm and I finished off whatever was left (often the sandwich and finishing the washing up.) I would then go straight to bed myself and sleep heavily in spite of the pain.

Time continued to race by and June was well under way. The second week of half term rolled on and my symptoms had begun to improve a little. I have not logged any extra concerns in my diary. Yet it was time for yet another sick note from the GP and I still could not walk well enough, I was still full of pain and permanently exhausted! When would it all end?

We were due to go on a family holiday to the Costa Brava on Saturday12th June 2004 and I did and did not want to go. I was worried about how I would manage with the MS abroad? What if I got worse?

What if this happened or that? Endless questions ran through my mind. Of course I wanted to enjoy the family time too so I felt torn. At the last House Group before we went away, members of the group prayed for me, for a good family holiday. One prayed that I would in fact improve whilst we were away and all agreed. Surprisingly, I thought it highly unlikely. I had sunk back down to being miserable once more. My husband still did not truly understand the MS and I felt he could not see the pain or understand the degree of difficulty involved. The House Group prayed and so did I, and hoped that God would answer.

He did answer! Even with my lack of belief, during the week we were away, after a few days I began to get a little stronger each day. There is nothing like watching the children happily playing on a beach anywhere. I discovered again, it really is true, that when the children are happy, you are happy too. On the last day, we went to the beach and with my husband's help I staggered into the sea and swam a few metres and then simply floated. I had not been able to do this for a long time. It felt so good and I felt safe with my husband's help. I felt the Lord really had answered those prayers.

Sunday 20th June I was back in Church with the boys. I was on the Welcome Team and it was amazing I was able to stand at the door and welcome people in for the twenty minutes or so before the service. I enjoyed it and it really helped me to stop thinking about myself and focus on others. The boys loved to be involved in giving out the weekly newsletter and of course people enjoyed that too. It gave me such a boost! I really looked forward to going.

On Tuesday 22nd June, Personnel visited me at home. I was still no closer to being back at work. I now realised I could do something, like be on the Welcome Team for twenty minutes one Sunday a month, but what good was that to an employer? I was still riddled with pain and exhaustion and it had now been for such a long time. I have recorded only that the meeting was alright, but no decisions appeared to have been made at that time.

I started with a sore throat that day which developed into earache too. When I saw a GP on Thursday, the Doctor decided it was viral so I received no antibiotics and simply had to wait for it to leave, on top of the MS symptoms. There was no time off for duties of being mum and housewife either. I felt really ill and trapped.

On Saturday26th, the boys stayed over with their Grandparents, which meant I could rest more. My husband went to work at his Sunday job. I stayed at home, as I was too ill to go to Church. On the Monday my sister Becky was due to be visiting with her youngest. I was still too ill, so my husband took Luke across to my sister's house, and I was able to rest at home some more. I believe another mum collected Peter from school for me.

We were now into July and I awoke one day to a new bout of increased numbness in the left hand side of my body. It was the first increase for some time, and it crept into my ankle up to my knee. "Was this the start of another relapse? Now what would happen?" It was the same pattern yet again.

Having picked up a little by Sunday 4th, I felt able to go to Church, where I enjoyed being on the Welcome Team once more. Sadly that evening, I began to feel feverish and had a rough night. It felt as though I shivered throughout the night, all my muscles twitched and I coughed for England! (Excessively) In the morning, breathing really hurt and I could not get out of bed. My husband called for the Doctor to visit. After a thorough examination she informed me I had Pleurisy! I thought that was something only the elderly got? I was prescribed antibiotics and anti-inflammatory pain killers. It had been necessary yet again, for my husband to take the day off work, to take Peter to school, look after Luke and take care of me.

The strongest memory of this time is how much my lungs hurt. I continued to be stuck in bed the next day. On the Wednesday my sore throat felt a little better as did my head. I had to take Peter to the school walking bus stop. This was just a few minutes from the house on the Mobility Scooter. I don't think I should have been out, but it was necessary for some reason. It hurt to breathe, but I prayed and God gave me what I needed and Peter was safe. My mother came that day and collected him from school and took him to the playground which he always enjoyed.

I must have found help with other mums, because I stayed in for the rest of the week. On Friday, school was closed with a teacher training day. Thankfully the childminder was able to have both boys so I was able to rest. On Saturday 10th July I began to recover from the Pleurisy. I rested again whilst my husband took the boys out for a day out at the Royal Armouries museum in Leeds. The next day my sister Becky and her family visited in the afternoon. My husband cooked a great tea for us all. I still felt ill but I have recorded that I was on the mend and I enjoyed spending time with my sister and all her family. As ever the children all enjoyed their cousins.

On Wednesday 14th I had a routine appointment at the Crohn's clinic in Leeds. My Father took me to the appointment. I had the joy of telling them about being healed of Crohn's disease in Jesus name. It was strange telling the truth, and they were pleased for my improved condition, yet you could see they had doubts. They did not offer to take me off their books. I did not insist they did so, either, as I was still feeling washed out with the Pleurisy. I decided that time would demonstrate that I was indeed healed of Crohn's Disease.

On Sunday 18th I finally felt well enough to go to Church, I felt weak, but so happy to go. The car broke down, so Rosie collected the boys and I in her car, and took us to Church. It felt so good to be back, as though I had been gone a long, long time. I was on the Welcome Team that day and have recorded that I sat down through the whole thing, as I was still weak, yet I enjoyed it.

On Tuesday 20th I saw the GP as my lungs still hurt and I still felt extra rough. The Pleurisy had now gone but my lungs remained inflamed. More rest was required, was the answer. How you are supposed to do that with two young children! Sometimes Doctor's say the most stupid things! The next day Sarah and her daughter Louise visited me. I had missed being able to spend time with them and going to the Church in Pontefract on Fridays. It was good to catch up with each other's news and laugh. On Friday 23rd July school closed for the summer holidays. I needed to hurry up and get better! My lungs continued to hurt for the rest of the month.

I had booked Luke an appointment at the Opticians, encouraged by my child-minder. Luke could not tell the difference between most colours and I wondered if he were colour blind? I had made the appointment at a local optician's which I could get to on the mobility scooter. The appointment was on 27th July. As he was so young, he sat on my knee for the eye test. I was completely taken by surprise at the end, when the Optician informed me that he had to refer Luke to the hospital eye clinic. He explained that there was a huge disparity between his left and right eye. So much so, Luke could hardly see out of his left eye and was likely not to be using it. He would need to wear glasses and would need investigating in case there was an underlying cause that required treatment. I pointed out that Luke had not stumbled or given any cause for concern regarding his eyesight. The Optician said it was likely he was born that way and knew no difference. This did not reassure me as a mum! I asked about the colour test and was told that a proper test could not be carried out until he was seven years old. The test he carried out showed likely partial colour blindness, but it was inconclusive. He assured me the hospital would be in contact with me directly and we left. My head was reeling, poor Luke. How would I manage to get him to hospital, and do whatever was needed when I could barely walk? I did not want him to suffer in any way whatsoever! Life felt so unjust!

19 - WORK

The next event was the very next day on Wednesday 28th July 2004, when there was a meeting at my home about my future. The boys spent the day with Grandparents. Personnel came, the Area Manager and my Trade Union Representative. Before this meeting I had been concerned about a number of things. My husband was not able to be there with me, because he had to be at work. I wanted him to be, as I felt so vulnerable and not capable enough. I prayed about the meeting and raised every one of my concerns with the Lord.

Just before the meeting my husband rang to wish me well. The previous night we had a long discussion where he made it clear he wanted me to return to work. I wanted to return to work! I tried to make it clear that I was not physically capable, because of all the MS symptoms. I remained so ill after all these months and my condition was still not improving. I think I was concerned by that point, I may not be able to have the opportunity, to go back to work.

Worryingly, my condition overall remained the same. I did my best to prepare myself for whatever was coming. I longed for my husband to see that I was in so much pain and the degree of numbness I had, that meant I was not capable of work. Yet he could not see the daily pain and struggle I had, and so I felt alone. For me, when he made that telephone call, I could see that he was really trying to be supportive. This made a huge impression on me and made me feel a little more hopeful.

The Area Manager and the woman from Personnel arrived first. Next came my Trade Union representative. I did not know him, but I was glad he was there to help and advise me.

I had worried that I may have to answer some awkward question, to which I did not know the answer? There was no such question asked. My Union Representative talked about the possibility of my being able to work from home, if for example I were to read newspapers for the blind. He spoke of a print shop in Headingley, and other such possibilities. "All great", I thought to myself, "If the pain, walking and exhaustion can just be sorted out."

They decided that a new Occupational Health assessment was required with a full medical. It could be the department's own Doctor or my own GP, who would give this full medical. It would take 8-10 weeks to complete this process. This meant longer to recover from the MS and the Pleurisy and hopefully feel a lot better.

Owing to the amount of time this would take, another request I had made of the Lord was answered. Luke was to begin part-time daily school nursery on an afternoon in September, and I really wanted to be able to take him myself, and settle him in to this new routine. I now knew I would be able to do so personally.

My employers extended my time on the redeployment programme by another three months, due to my willingness to seek work. I felt there could be another job opportunity available to me, if I were indeed to recover. I thanked the Lord after this meeting because He had answered my every concern. It came as a pleasant surprise to me that God could care about every little thing that concerned me. I had learned of his love of people over the years, and of course He had healed me of the Crohn's Disease, which was amazing! I did not understand what He was doing now? Why had He not healed me yet? What did it all mean? Of one thing I felt certain, that He must truly love me and so I hung on to that.

On Friday 30th July, my husband and I went to London with the boys for a weekend, staying at my eldest Cousins home. He and his partner, blessed us with a lovely weekend of sightseeing, including a trip on an Amphibious Tour on the Thames River which both boys absolutely loved! We all really enjoyed ourselves. I did wonder how I would manage? Yet I coped better than I had imagined, and enjoyed myself in spite of the MS symptoms and pain. I could not climb up the twisting stairs to the top of the bus, but that seemed to be the only restriction I faced that day. The next day they treated us to a trip to 'Legoland' which we all enjoyed. It was so good to see the boys so happy, and my husband too. Both of them truly showered us with their kindness and blessed us all, with a much needed break.

The holidays were in full swing and I continued to do my best to keep the boys happy and entertained, whilst coping with the MS.

We had a family get together, with a picnic in a park in Dewsbury. My parents took us together and the boys as ever, enjoyed fun with their cousins, whilst my husband was at work. I was always asked the same questions by family and friends alike, and it would disturb me when I was giving the same answer I gave several months ago. I desperately wanted to be well, yet I did not know when I would get well? I seemed never any closer to being well. Any improvements I had, seemed but fleeting. There were so many things wrong with me, I did not know what should be dealt with first. I simply wanted this whole nightmare to come to an end. But I never awoke, this was my life now.

My GP issued yet another sick note, as my symptoms remained the same. I was still unable to walk well enough to work. The pain continued to dominate my waking moments, and I still focused on making it through each day, and escaping the pain through sleep each night. In mid-August I had some improvement with increased feeling in my legs and feet. My hands improved a little too. Yet I had by now, stopped pinning all my hopes on slight improvements. Complete healing never arrived, and I dare not hope any longer that this was it, as I had found it extremely disappointing, every time that had not been the case.

At the Healing School, I knew that I needed to have some one-to- one Christian counselling from Joe King and his wife Suzi. When the Lord healed me so dramatically of Crohn's Disease, it was truly incredible! Everything covered at that time in the teaching spoke directly to me. It was as though that teaching session had been created with me in mind. It took some time for me to absorb all that had happened and be ready to move on to individual time with them. I contacted them subsequently, and received a detailed questionnaire in the post to complete, all about my significant life history and that of my parents.

My first appointment to see them was on 24th August. My mother collected the boys and I, and entertained the boys, whilst I was with Joe and Suzi. They were living 'by faith' at that time. This meant neither of them had a fixed income from a regular job. They of course needed food to eat and money to pay all the bills, but trusted God to provide for them one day at a time and He did. At that time they asked for a donation for each session. There were two of them giving me two hours each of their time and I gave them thirty pounds for this. It sounds incredibly stingy when I write this, but it was all I felt I could manage at that time, and they were thankful for my donation. When I think of Plumbers and other tradespersons, I should really have paid them double. They began to make a positive difference, even in this first session going over my life history.

I had completed a questionnaire all about my life history and the 'fear' pattern was revealed. Of course I knew I had always been afraid of people, but I did not see how this fear controlled and tormented me so much over the years.

I discovered with Joe and Suzi, this fear began with the eye surgery I had, when I was eighteen months old. The Surgeon decided I would have the operation without anaesthetic! I was held down for the procedure, whilst my tear ducts were opened. Consequently, I was afraid of everyone except my mother.

I had not made close friends with my peers due to the 'fear'. I also found I as I grew up, I did not enjoy pop music and make-up that other girls my age enjoyed. This meant I was really a loner. I did try to fit in at times, but gave it up.

I had been bullied at school when I was eleven years old, in particular by two girls in the year above me at middle school. I could not handle it, and they walked all over me for approximately nine months. My parents and other family members would always tell me to stand up for myself, but I simply could not find the strength. I received little pocket money then, but what little I had they took, as well as numerous tennis balls I played 'two-ball' with. One day I had no money left and had not been able to replace the balls. When these two girls cornered me, pushed and threatened me as usual, I found myself getting cross. I remember telling them that I had no money, and would not replace any more balls, as they took them away and I had lived through more than enough! I was really surprised those words came out of my mouth. I was also surprised when the response was that I did have some spunk after all! They left me alone from that moment on! I was relieved it was over, but mad with myself that it had taken me so long to achieve it!

I moved on to High School and was still largely unhappy, with no close friends. I did have a number of friends but not a close one in any of my classes. I was still afraid of people, although I had realised by now that nothing terrible generally happened. I did finally make friends with a non-judgmental boy I bumped into one lunch-time. He and I shared the same kind of humour. We kept in touch for approximately five years after school and I have very happy memories of this time. Unfortunately, I introduced him to Frank and this meant I found our relationship difficult after my devastating loss. Our great friendship became a painful reminder for me from this point on, so I allowed us to drift apart.

Of course Joe and Suzi knew about the rape, although I had to fill in the detail as I have done here. I also had to explain more about my relationship with Frank, in order for them to fully understand. I wanted there to be an A, B, C, method that would lead to my being well once more. Of course there wasn't one. However, they gave me hope, a strong sense that all was not lost and that was priceless! During this first session the main thing that came across was my poor self-image. I had to begin work on changing my mind set. One thing I recorded from this session was that when Joe prayed, he felt God saying that I had to let myself off the hook. "How do I do that?" I thought to myself. So first of all, I learned to say it out loud.

On Friday 27th August I saw a GP and began a new medicine for the MS. This one was called Amitriptyline. It had originally been developed for depression but was later discovered to be very good at dealing with Neuropathic Pain which I was overflowing with. I had tried Gabapentin already which had no effect. I tried it on various doses over a number of months and eventually my body reacted against it. I had become allergic to Penicillin aged six. I had continued to react against various medicines over the years. My body was definite about what it would and would not allow. I usually got a rash and felt feverish and headachy. I would often become nauseous too. All these symptoms would go away once I came off the offending medicine. There was some degree of difficulty initially because the Consultant was largely seen to be taking care of me and so my medicine was left to him. However it was several months in between each Consultation. This felt far too long, and so I eventually asked the GP if they could prescribe something that I could try, at least until I next saw the Consultant. I was thinking by this time that surely there must be a medicine out there that would suit me? I started on 10 mg of Amitriptyline that day. It appeared to make no immediate difference, but I felt empowered for the first time, by trying something else to end the constant tormenting pain.

The following day we went as a family to a Leisure pool. I left my stick at the edge of the pool to walk into the water. I found it very intimidating without full feeling in my legs and feet. The floor looked so hard and I knew it would hurt should I fall. The children ran in laughing away with their Dad in hot pursuit. I had to face my fears on my own, balance on what were supposedly my legs, and slowly make them carry me into the water. I have continued over these years to find large spaces threatening. There was the lack of things to grab should I stumble and so it felt really vulnerable.

At this swimming pool they had a type of flume water slide, with a plunge pool at the bottom. I was able to leave my stick at the bottom and climb the stairs with the boys to go down this slide. My husband went first with Peter on his knee. I followed behind with Luke on mine. When we hit the plunge pool I immediately went completely under the water and so did Luke on my knee. I almost panicked as for a moment I could not find my feet and the right way up to stand and Luke was under the water too. "Why had I not thought sufficiently about this before I went down? What kind of thoughtless mother did that make me?" I was able to stand quite quickly and grab a spluttering Luke who had got a shock on going under the water, just as I had. My husband had managed to land on his feet and hold Peter up so he did not get totally immersed. He had already got out of the plunge pool with Peter and returned to the swimming pool. I realised the MS meant I should not be going down such apparatus. I had to think things through better as well. Luke was shocked but thankfully got over the shock very quickly and was soon happily playing once more with his brother and Dad. I felt a hopeless failure, not able to perform properly as a person or a mother. I was very hard on myself. I would not let myself go on such a slide again.

On 2nd September 2004, my medical health assessment finally arrived. A taxi had been booked to take me to see the Doctor they were employing to assess me in Leeds. I was nervous, "What if he could not see the pain I was in, as my husband could not? What if I could not answer a question?" I over analysed the whole scenario. When I arrived at this large building I was advised which floor and room to go to. When I arrived no-one was there. I waited a while and then looked for someone. I was directed to the correct administrative staff and discovered that the Doctor was not well himself. Apparently someone had tried to call me on the telephone but the number they had, bore no relation to mine. I simply had to sit and wait for the returning taxi to take me back home. I felt bad for my employer as it was a half hour journey by taxi each way, which would be expensive. I hoped it would not be long before it was rearranged.

On Saturday 4th September, another of my cousin's was getting married. This meant a car journey with the boys down south. My Aunt had kindly loaned us the use of her house towards Oxford. We travelled into the countryside, to find the historical looking house which was the beautiful venue. As parents of two young children, we only just made it on time as there were a number of false starts. It did not help when my husband and I both thought that the other had picked up the wedding clothes still hanging up in the house! The wedding was lovely, but I felt so trapped. I could not stand around and talk with others, my body would not do it. Instead I had to keep going to sit down before I fell down. After the ceremony, the children all went into the large gardens. Once my husband and I discovered how safe they were, we were able to leave them to really enjoy themselves. I felt I was not able to do this myself, because I was in so much pain. It was as though the pain were devouring me. I tried to focus on the occasion but I really struggled. I did not want my life to be this way. I wanted to truly enjoy family gatherings like this one. Yet I was not in a position to do anything about it. The muscle pain increased during that day and I was unhappy, although I did my best not to show it. It felt like an endurance test.

On 5th September it was Peter's birthday he was now 6 years old. I was shocked that there I was celebrating another birthday with him, when I still had as much pain as a year ago! Yet I loved him dearly, so I sought to make his day as special as possible, along with his Dad. We travelled back home that day. When we got home I was able to make a Doctor's appointment for the next day. The Doctor I saw increased the Amitriptyline to 20mg per day. There was still no change in my symptoms.

On 7th September I had my second appointment with Joe King. I found it hard openly discussing all my past. I need not have worried, as he and Suzi were always supportive and encouraging. It was just me, focusing on me. Yet it had become apparent I needed to deal with the past effectively, in order to move into a happier state of mind in the future at the very least.

That day they gave me Exodus 23:30 which they felt was for me. In this passage of the Bible the Lord speaks to the Israelites and says he will not drive out all the enemies at once, as the land would be deserted, and the animals would be too many for them to handle. Instead he said that I will drive them out little by little, until you are stronger, (my paraphrase). I did not like little by little, I wanted to be healed now! I wanted this nightmare to come to an end quickly. Yet it was obvious this was not going to be the case.

I was also asked about my mother who had suffered greatly as a child during WWII. She was the youngest daughter of parents who were British Christian Missionaries in China. Born in China she remembers the Sino Japanese War before WW11when she was between the ages of 4-7. During this war the Japanese planes flew overland during the day and night. Sometimes she would be walking in the fields with her parents when they would hear the droning noise of the approaching planes. They would quickly seek cover under a bridge, or wherever cover could be found, as she witnessed sharp shooting from the planes. My mother said she found this very disturbing, especially if someone was shot. At night when the Japanese planes attacked, they had to go into a dug out underground shelter, made with a roof covered in tree branches. Her mother would always quote Proverbs 18:10 "The name of the Lord is a strong tower, the Godly run to it and they are safe." Those words proved true time and again.

When she was seven years old in 1940, she went to an International Boarding School for the children of missionaries in China. There she was to join her older sister, a long way from home in Chefoo. Her parent's home was in a place called Chungo near Sien in the Shensi province. From there it took a whole month to travel to Chefoo. Mum remembers travelling mostly by train. Both parents accompanied her and when they arrived, they enjoyed family time for a week in the mission home with her older sister. This was the last time my mother saw her father. The following year whilst she was at boarding school he contracted Typhus and died.

The Second World War broke out whilst she was at boarding school in Chefoo, and things began to change. In 1942 after Pearl Harbour, the British were considered enemies of the state to the occupying Japanese. All the children at the school were issued with armbands donating their nationality. The Japanese wanted the large school site which had three school buildings and a mission home so they all had to move into much smaller premises outside Chefoo where they were kept under armed guard. They had roll call every day and the children all had to learn to count to ten in Japanese. They were there for 10 months.

In the summer of 1943 the whole school were taken hundreds of miles away by boat, possibly train, and then truck to Weihsien. On the way the teachers and children kept their spirits up by singing "God is still on the throne, and he will remember his own. Though trials may press us, and burdens distress us, he never will leave us alone. His promise is true he will never forget you, God is still on the throne." My mother says the teachers were marvellous, in the selfless way they looked after the children. They even ran their own 'Brownie' club.

At Weihsien, they lived in an Internment Camp. The Preparatory School which mum lived in was in one building. Her sister in the Girls High School, was on the other side of the camp, whilst the Japanese Soldiers and prisoners lived in yet another part of the camp. Each section was divided off. Roll calls were made every morning and evening. My mother lived in fear there like most, although there were a few children who saw the experience as an adventure. She has shared how frightening it was when bombs were dropped by the allies. In Camp my mother met Eric Liddell who was also a prisoner, he taught the children how to play basketball. She remembers him as being a very kind man. Sadly during the time at camp he died of a brain tumour.

My mother was and remains afraid of Alsatian dogs, which the guards used to constantly patrol around the perimeter of the camp. The Japanese allowed the camp to be run by the residents of the camp and she feels it was run well, and so it was a better prison than many others experienced in China. My mum also feels strongly, that they were helped by the vast number of people she learned of, who were praying for them.

Hunger was a constant problem in camp. The Japanese ate just two meals a day and so they provided two meals for all in the camp. My mother remembers these were divided up by staff into three small meals each day. They were poor in quality and only occasionally contained meat of suspicious origin. They all subsequently suffered with malnutrition. She remembers that wild sunflowers grew and she and a friend would pick and eat the seeds, without realising they were enjoying a little protein.

Many of the children came out in boils and other sicknesses as a result of the malnutrition. There was little that staff could do to help. My mother's sister became seriously ill with Osteomyletis of her hip, on the journey home after the war as a direct result of malnutrition. Thankfully she was saved in part by the use of the new antibiotic Penicillin. The Camp was eventually liberated by the Americans at the end of the war. The Japanese commander committed suicide at this time, as he felt it was dishonourable for him to have failed in his position. The Japanese at that time placed great emphasis on 'honour'.

My mother had spent 4 years imprisoned, yet felt that although life in the Internment Camp was so difficult and frightening, God was good to her through it all. The teachers worked hard with the children at giving them the best possible time they could. Mum even says that the Lord has never stopped making it up to her, in all the years she has lived since.

I did not think that what had happened to my mother could have any bearing on me until that session with Joe and Suzi. Joe questioned me about my views of the Japanese. I did not think I really had any views. However when Joe called out for any Spirit present in me of a Japanese Soldier, my body suddenly reacted as though a bolt of electricity had gone through it. I was really surprised by this and concerned by what it meant? After more prayer and commanding of spirits to leave, Joe asked me to lift my hands and praise Jesus and then suddenly, I felt like a rod went down the back of my throat beyond my stomach. This rod forced my head back and I sat up rigid in the chair. Joe took authority and in righteous anger swung his arm down in front of me declaring "I break the rod in the power of Jesus name." I felt it break in half physically! I shouted, "It's broken!" Joe commanded it shatter into tiny pieces and leave my body on my breath in Jesus name and I felt it do just that, and pictured it in my head. It was truly amazing! I had felt afraid when the rod pinned me to the chair, but when the rod broke and then shattered in Jesus name, I felt elated and all fear was gone! They then both prayed and filled me up with God's joy and other blessings. They also prayed for my protection until we met next time. The pins and needles always increased after being prayed over. I learned this was just a temporary increase over time, and did my best not to fear about what might happen next, although I was not very good at it at that time.

I saw Joe and Suzi usually once a fortnight initially, then monthly and sometimes less often for nearly three years in total. They sought to teach me Biblical principles I had somehow missed. They prayed fervently over me. They evicted demons and filled me with God's love and blessed me a great deal. It was so good to spend time with them! I cannot truly express what a positive impact they had on me and how thankful I am for all their prayers and hard work. One verse Joe would often quoted was Hosea 4:6, "My people are dying through lack of knowledge." They both felt this was true of me and gradually I saw it too, and sought to rectify this.

I had prayers to say, to help me to forgive myself and let myself off the hook. One such prayer was;

'Thank you Lord, for forgiving me for things that I have thought, said and done which are wrong and for which I am truly sorry. I now choose to forgive myself, for the things that I know you have already forgiven me for. I accept and forgive myself for all my shortcomings. I believe that my sin is no sooner confessed than forgiven. I believe that you have placed all my sins at the bottom of the deepest ocean and put up a "No Fishing" sign. Thank you Jesus.' I said this prayer time and again as I realised I had not forgiven me. It became a favourite of mine because God's forgiveness never ceased to amaze me. It was through them I first learned to speak God's Word out loud, and also to appreciate what I had.

I was given a number of Bible verses to read and think on, to encourage me and help my faith to grow. Some such verses were;

"Even the very hairs on your head are all numbered. So do not fear as you are of greater worth than many sparrows." Luke 12:7

"For God has not given us a spirit of fear and timidity, but of power, love, and self-discipline." 2Timothy 1:7

"Long ago, even before he made the world, God loved us, and chose us in Christ to be holy and without fault in his eyes." Ephesians 1:4

"My gracious favour is all you need. My power works best in your weakness." 2Corinthians 12:8

"For I know the plans I have for you," says the Lord. "They are plans for good and not for disaster, to give you a future and a hope. In those days when you pray, I will listen. If you look for me in earnest, you will find me when you seek me. I will be found by you." Jeremiah 29:11

I enjoyed looking up each of the verses after the session. It helped me to see the truth of God's love, learn and slowly grow in faith.

The following week the muscle pain in my body increased it seemed, every day. I saw one of my Consultant's team on Thursday 16th September. This male staff member felt I should give Gabapentin another try. He was quite insistent and so I eventually agreed. By the end of the week the numbness had increased in both my left and right foot. On Monday 20th I fell down. I have not stated where, but have blamed taking Gabapentin in my records. I visited Joe and his wife the next day and then in the evening I was ill with vomiting. My husband took Wednesday off work to take care of me and the boys whilst I began to recover. The pain in my legs decreased that day. This brought unexpected relief. My legs felt sore, as though I had worked too hard at a Gym the previous day.

I managed to get a Doctor's appointment for Thursday 23rd. This Dr. prescribed the anti-histamine 'Piriton', for what he felt was an allergic reaction to the Gabapentin. I did not take Gabapentin anymore but began the anti-histamine. I said lots of 'stupid Doctor' under my breath for the trainee Consultant at the hospital, and told myself I was stupid too, for being persuaded to give Gabapentin another try. My leg muscles remained sore for another few days. I had to hurry up and recover as my husband had booked a last minute cheap holiday for the four of us to Crete.

We flew from Manchester on 28th September to Crete. My husband had assured me that he had informed the holiday firm of my walking difficulties so he felt sure everything would be taken care of. Sadly, this was not the case. We had booked a two bedroomed apartment but when we arrived this was up two flights of external concrete stairs! The stairs were broken into four segments and had no hand rails. It was so dangerous for me, as well as painful. The man who ran the apartments was not there when we first arrived. My husband had to collect the key from somewhere first. I was so disappointed, and could not imagine being able to climb those stairs each day, both in terms of energy and being able to balance safely. The apartment itself was fine. Had I a wheelchair, I believe I would have been able to use it within the apartment but I did not have one there and neither did they have lift access! I did not know what to do and cried with tears of frustration and disappointment that my needs had not been taken into account and I was in so much pain!

My husband thankfully rang the holiday operator and told her the apartment was just not suitable and pointed out that he had passed on the information of my walking difficulties. The information given was apparently not enough to arrange the correct accommodation was the response. The man who ran the apartment block was contacted and duly arrived.

He had been aware I had some walking difficulties too, but did not know what that meant and had only that two bedroom apartment available. He offered us either or both of the one bedroomed apartments on the ground floor. We went to view them and chose the larger of the two for our week's stay. It was effectively a bedsit with two beds. Yet at least we were all together. We learned that my needs had to be spelt out in detail, wherever we went from that time on.

In spite of the problems, we enjoyed the holiday. I enjoyed watching the boys swim in the nearby hotel with a pool. I just went in once, as the water was so cold and I discovered that cold water made the muscles in my legs go into painful spasms which left me unable to stand. That was frightening at the time. I found I was unable to swim as a result and when I got to the side of the pool I was not able to get out. My husband had to lift me out of the pool. I did not understand what was happening in my body at this time. I simply focused on the two cute and happy little boys, swimming about in their armbands. They really were a lifeline to me, and I thanked the Lord for them. I found the holiday a mixture of hard work, enduring the endless pain, and yet pleasurable because of the boys. 'If the pain could just be brought under control it would make such a difference', I thought to myself many, many times. Daily life was such a struggle and I was tired of struggling. We came home without any further MS difficulties and life continued.

20 - Regeneration of the Optic Nerve

I should have felt happy and blessed. I had been abroad twice in one year and I had two gorgeous boys. Yet I did not feel happy as I was consumed with pain and I was so tired. I was tired mentally and physically. I kept pushing myself to keep the boys happy, to keep the house ticking over, but it wasn't enough. My husband and I were distant with each other. We were both still confused and stressed by the MS and all the problems it brought. When would things change for the better?

On 9th October 2004, Joe King had a healing concert at St. Matthias Church in Leeds. Sarah was not able to go and I desperately wanted the chance to be prayed over. I mentioned it to a few of my Church family and Pam offered to take me. I was overjoyed, although a little concerned as it meant a lot of driving for her. Pam insisted she would like to take me and so I went willingly. We both enjoyed all the worship, then I clearly remember praying to the Lord. At that point I was kneeling. I felt Jesus was close by me, even though

I could not see anything physically, I could sense His presence. I reached out with my right hand as I felt I could not cope any longer with the MS. I needed help. I felt Him take my hand and hold it. I do not know how long this time lasted. I felt as though I could have just stayed there forever, as He somehow poured more mental strength into me.

Pam then called me, as Joe wanted to pray over me at the front with others. I went forward for prayer and although my physical symptoms did not change, all my anxiety left and I felt so much stronger mentally and so more able to cope. Pam then blessed me as she too had been praying for me, whilst in her seat. The Lord had said to her that every time the word MS cropped up in my head, I was to say "My Saviour". I was not to be pulled down by the letters MS, any longer but think 'My Saviour' every single time. As I thought about it, I saw the truth in it. The word 'MS' had a miserable, ominous strength in my head. I certainly said lots of 'Stupid MS' in my head. I worked hard at this to change my thought life.

I was kept uplifted for a few days and then the pain wore me down once more. On Thursday 14th it was the night before my 35th birthday and the same old frustrations surfaced over trying to celebrate, whilst being so exhausted and in so much pain. Not only that, but I was due to go to the eye clinic yet again. Before I got into bed, I poured it all out to the Lord in prayer. I would have to go on the bus on my own and I did not feel stable enough. I would be at the eye clinic for 2-3 hours as this was usual. Worse still, they would put stinging eye drops in that blurred your vision for the rest of the day and they could not help me anyway! I was still wearing sunglasses all the time for the light sensitivity I gained in August 2003. I ended my prayer by saying if He could make something good come out of it, that would be good, as I was so low. As I got into bed, little did I know, I was about to discover how God loves honest prayers from the heart.

It was my 35th birthday and the numbness had increased again. My husband was at home that day, we got the boys ready and then he did the school run, whilst I left for the hospital. The bus journey went smoothly without the driver causing any lurching, or any other incident. I arrived at the clinic and was surprised to be called in to see a different Consultant in less than an hour. I thought they must have made a mistake as no one had come to me with eye drops. I voiced my concern of the possible mistake. The Consultant said he had some fast acting, short term drops he would use, that lasted for just two hours and promptly put them in. He then examined both of my eyes and completed all the usual tests thoroughly. This included my reading letters and looking through books identifying numbers hidden within dots etc. At the end of this he sat at his desk and threw his pen down. What was he doing I wondered? He exclaimed "I don't believe it, I just don't believe it. It is simply not possible!" I had no idea what he was talking about. Yet I will never forget his incredulity. I could sense he would say more so I waited. "Is this a special day for you or something?" he asked. "Yes it's my birthday." I replied. "Well I have some birthday good news for you" he said. I wondered what on earth he was going to say? He paused and then continued, "I have just examined you and completed all the usual tests you have had for more than a year now. Yet you now have 98% perfect vision in both of your eyes. This is not possible, because the Optic Nerve does not regenerate! But yours has, and I do not understand it!"

At times I am not quick to grasp things, and many people do not realise how the MS makes it much harder to think. I did not truly understand what he meant. He explained more, "Tests have been carried out on your eyes since you first came to us in August 2003. The first attack of the MS caused the Optic Nerve to die in your left eye. The same eye tests have been carried out on you each time you have been here. And now today's test results show that you have 98% perfect vision in both eyes!" I still did not truly understand what he was saying to me but I thanked him anyway.

I wondered why I still had light sensitivity in my eyes, if I had 98% perfect vision and so I asked him. He surprised me by saying he did not know why I had that in the first place? He passed me the appointment sheet to book my next visit with reception so I knew it was time to get up and leave. As I left the room he was repeatedly saying, "It does not make sense. It is impossible, the Optic Nerve does not regenerate. It's just not possible!"

I walked to the reception desk to make the next appointment and had to wait in a queue. There were two or three ahead of me. Whilst I waited I kept thinking of all the Consultant had said. His words played over and over in my mind and then all of a sudden the penny dropped and I suddenly realised that the Lord had healed my Optic Nerve. Not only had he done that, but he had answered every single thing I had raised with Him in my prayer the previous night. He had started by ensuring the bus journey went well with a driver who drove carefully with consideration for the passengers. I did not have the usual stinging eye drops put into my eyes that blur your vision all day. I was seen by the Consultant after less than an hour's wait, so I wasn't there the usual 2-3 hours. It was totally amazing what He had done and that He had answered when I prayed. I had prayed fed up and totally honestly; "If you can bring anything good out of it that would be good." He had answered every item on my list and given me the most incredible birthday gift ever!

When I realised the truth of this, I started beaming from ear to ear! It was suddenly my turn at reception and the member of staff had to get my attention. She commented on my big smile, then spoke about the next appointment. I did not feel able to share my joy! I did not want anyone to spoil it! I was elated, the journey home slipped smoothly by and I enjoyed the best birthday ever, from the minute the penny dropped. The God who created the Universe had healed my Optic Nerve! He had answered my prayer, my despondent honest prayer! Wow! I can still hear to this day, the Consultant in my head saying, "It's not possible, the Optic Nerve does not regenerate. I do not understand, It's just not possible." I was overjoyed! I felt I did not understand why? Why would God answer that prayer? Whatever the reason, it was so good! Yet I could not help but wonder why He did not heal me completely? Yet I refused to let that bother me, but chose to focus on the joy of that experience instead.

I still had MS and yet God had healed my Optic Nerve! It was beyond amazing and I just knew, even more strongly than before, that my God would heal me completely. I did not understand what God was doing, but I knew nothing was impossible for Him, he had done the miraculous in me again! This was far from the end of my healing journey. I knew the best was yet to come!